Russian Illuminated Manuscripts

Olga Popova

RUSSIAN ILLUMINATED MANUSCRIPTS

with 69 illustrations, 48 in color

Thames and Hudson

Translated from the Russian by
Kathleen Cook, Vladimir Ivanov and Lenina Sorokina

First published in the USA in 1984 by Thames and Hudson Inc.,
500 Fifth Avenue, New York, New York 10110

Library of Congress Catalog Card Number 83-70804

Printed and bound in Denmark

Introduction

It is the aim of this study to reveal an almost unknown world of art concealed within the heavy bindings of Russian medieval manuscripts. Most of these luxurious books were created for churches or monasteries, and the few that were made for lay patrons were usually commissioned for motives of piety; all, therefore, contain texts of Christian content.

The Russian princes accepted Christianity as the religion of their State in the tenth century as a result of a period of intense missionary activities on the part of the Byzantine Church of Constantinople. (Vladimir, prince of Kiev, is traditionally said to have accepted Orthodox baptism in 988.) Since Christianity was brought to Russia from Byzantium, the Russian Church followed the Byzantine model, and this influence is at its clearest in the forms of its liturgy and the development of its art. Any study of early Russian culture therefore entails comparison with Byzantine forms of expression, and the recognition of subtle differences, particularly during the period from the fourteenth to the sixteenth centuries, when the centralization of the Russian State in Moscow stimulated the development of a national identity. The slow and subtle development of a new form of manuscript illumination is the subject of this study, and is documented in the selection of miniatures chosen for the illustrations.

The earliest Russian illuminated books to have survived are from the eleventh century. They are large, and are written on parchment; the texts are surrounded by broad margins, and the script is in the forms known either as uncial or semi-uncial. The written language of Russian Christians was Old Church Slavonic, and the alphabet was cyrillic; uncial manuscripts use capital letters (majuscules) throughout, and the semi-uncial script is an adaptation to a more cursive form. The illuminated pages are in vivid, rich colours, and the combination of miniatures and ornament with the well-spaced script creates the characteristic appearance of Russian manuscripts – dignity and clarity. These contrast with one kind of manuscript popular in Byzantium, where the pictures are surrounded by closely written minuscules and intricate ornaments. On the whole, it might be said that Russian books are more direct and less refined than the best productions of Constantinople.

Russian miniatures are usually large in scale, filling the whole page. Author-portraits are one of the most frequent subjects – David at the beginning of a Psalter, Prophets and Apostles in Bibles, and the Four Evangelists in Gospel books. Sometimes, however, the illuminations take the form of small scenes that illustrate the text symbolically or literally. These are placed in the margins of illuminated psalters, or between the lines of script in lives of the saints or historical chronicles.

Early miniatures possess great charm and display craftsmanship of an extremely high level. They are also of exceptional value for the study of medieval art, since they can often be dated precisely, and have survived in better condition than other forms of painting. Moreover, they occasionally throw light on periods from which no frescoes or icons have survived.

Ornament of a variety of kinds also plays a considerable part in the embellishment of Russian manuscripts. It may be sumptuous and brilliant, as in Byzantine manuscripts, glittering like enamels or precious stones, or have a fanciful quality, with a lavish use of decorative initials.

Early Russian Christian art, including manuscript illumination, begins in Kiev in the eleventh century. For several centuries thereafter, Russian art represented a mixture of Byzantine and local features. In the eleventh- and twelfth-century art of Kiev, specifically Russian types of form and craftsmanship have been detected, and have been seen as the first departures from Byzantine models. The schemes of Byzantine art were modified, and pictures grew more imposing as the visual language grew simpler. Miniatures of this period reflect the variety of tastes among Kievan patrons.

We find an example of the Byzantine sources of Russian illumination in the earliest extant Russian illuminated manuscript, the Ostromir Lectionary, produced in 1056–7 in Kiev. The first miniature, of St John with St Prochoros (Pl. 1), is close in style to the illuminations of Byzantine manuscripts. The elegant quatrefoil frame, the types of ornament, the tiled floor, the finely drawn lion, the abundance of gold and rich colours, the style of the painting, with broad highlights representing light and delicate coloured shadows in the folds, are all features that recall the richness, refinement and sumptuousness of the art of contemporary Byzantium.

Two other miniatures from the same manuscript (St Mark and St Luke, Pl. 2) seem to be the work of a different illuminator, and are painted in a manner reminiscent of enamels, which were very popular in Kiev at that

i The Sviatoslav
Codex
(for detailed
information,
see pp. 29–30)

time. The outlines are rendered in gold, and the mesh of gold lines
neutralizes the solid colour of the robes.

We find a regional variation of the Byzantine style in the Mstislav
Lectionary, produced between 1103 and 1117 in Novgorod (iii–iv, Pls. 3–5).
The Ostromir Lectionary was so highly valued and well known that the
miniatures became a model for imitation. The Mstislav Lectionary shows
its direct influence; yet, while miniatures and ornament reproduce almost
exactly their Kievan models (retaining the general composition of the
leaves, the quatrefoil frames, the architectural backgrounds, the patterns of
the tiled floors, the Byzantine ornament and the iconography), the nature

of the images and the style of the illustrations display the characteristic features of early Novgorodian art. These features may be defined as a sharp angularity, and a heightened power and inner tension of the figures that produce an immediate, strong impact on the viewer.

The representational devices used here are simple and accessible, in the Novgorodian style. The illuminator likes complex effects, relying not on harmony but on contrast. His forms are large and heavy, and he throws highlights on the faces sharply and accurately – a style of painting also found in the Novgorod frescoes that survive from this period. The structure is provided by the spare, firm drawing. The colours reveal what may be Novgorodian taste – they are clear and bright, laid on side by side, separately, not blending. The illuminator's fondness for the coloured drawing, for expressiveness of line and vivid, decorative colouring, is characteristic. Such a style lacks refinement but is attractive in its directness, freshness and richness.

In the course of the twelfth century and early decades of the thirteenth, up to the time of the Mongol invasion of 1237–8, Kiev declined, and the period is marked historically by the division of Russia into independent principalities. With this division came the development of local art centres that were the heirs to Kievan art. It can be argued that these new urban centres developed their own traditions, and distinctive manners of painting.

Most of the illuminated manuscripts of this pre-Mongolian period which have survived are from north Russia, and all date from the latter part of the twelfth or from the early thirteenth century. Most belong to a single group, similar in the style of their script and illumination. There is some evidence that they were all produced in Rostov, in the same workshop, and belonged to Bishop Cyril of Rostov. A chronicle tells us that he possessed an extensive library, on whose shelves an Acts of the Apostles of 1220 (Pl. 7) once stood. The miniature of the Apostles Peter and Paul, large, bright and colourful, with elongated, slender figures and sumptuous, heavy ornament, is reminiscent in its richness and splendour of the princely books of Kiev. This style of painting, with its restrained softness and lack of tension in the figures, is characteristic of the art of such Russian cities as Vladimir, Suzdal, Rostov and Yaroslavl. The figures in this miniature possess a particular radiance. Although all the forms are elongated, their outlines and contours are calm and natural. The colours are light, and the robes are pierced with faint, almost

ii The Sviatoslav
Codex

imperceptible white lines, symbolizing light. The robes seem airy, the figures ethereal, disembodied and hovering, and the whole composition has an aura of spirituality and refinement. These qualities were to predominate in Moscow painting in the fourteenth century, and became the basis of the style of the great painter Andrei Rublev. The source of these qualities is to be found in Byzantine art of the eleventh and twelfth centuries: the works of icon painters from Constantinople were known in Russia; for example in twelfth-century Vladimir a famous Byzantine icon of the Virgin was venerated, and Byzantine artists worked in the church of St Demetrius there. Certainly the Byzantine art of Constantinople contributed to the development of the regional art named Rostov-Suzdalian, and indeed, of the art of the whole of north-east Russia. Here Byzantine modes of expression were reinterpreted, and painting acquired a specifically Russian cast, lacking to a certain extent in classical harmony, and with a greater softness.

Byzantine models were differently interpreted in the workshops of the Galich-Volynian Principality, a rich and flourishing region in the thirteenth century, with many towns, a distinctive style of architecture, and extensive contacts with the Byzantine world and Western Europe. Minia-

iii The Mstislav
Lectionary

tures are the only works to have survived from the early pre-Mongolian period in the Galich-Volynian area. They include four leaves portraying the Evangelists in a Lectionary of the early thirteenth century (Pl. 9). Although tiny, the miniatures possess great expressiveness with heavily modelled figures, so that they seem as powerful as fresco painting. Everything about them appears exaggerated, hardly in keeping with the scale of a miniature. The manner of execution of the Galich miniatures is new, and unlike that of Byzantine and Russian works of the eleventh and twelfth centuries. It is as if, instead of 'dematerializing' and spiritualizing form, the illuminator is striving to capture objects in all their density and volume. The robes of the Evangelists are rich and heavy, draped in numerous thick folds, with an abundance of vivid white highlights. Modelling and texture are all-important. There are scarcely any gradations of colour, and all the colours are strong. In order to convey space, the artist presents architecture and objects – chairs, stools and tables – in perspective. This treatment is new in Russian painting, although close to Byzantine art of the thirteenth century. The miniatures of the Galich manuscript are evidence of a considerable Russian artistic revival, and point to Russian participation in a process common to all the countries of the Byzantine world.

In Russia, this process of development was to be cut short by the Mongol invasion. Russian art of the middle and latter part of the thirteenth

iv The Mstislav
Lectionary

v The Dobrilovo
Gospels

century, the period of Mongol occupation, broke away, as the weakening
of contacts with the outside world diverted it to a different path. It reflected
an altered attitude to life, a different understanding of the meaning of
images, a different view, even, of the possibilities of art. In this period a
bright, flat style predominated, rather coarse, rather heavy in execution,
simplified, and of an almost hypnotic power. Dynamism of form was
replaced by a static representation; exaltation by aloofness, plasticity by
abstraction and a decorative simplification of form. Architectural settings
gave way to coloured backgrounds that excluded any sense of space and
surroundings. Paintings, including the miniature, became simpler and
more severely ascetic. These changes in the treatment of the image affected
the whole of Russian art. The difference between the illuminated manuscripts of the pre-Mongolian period and those of the Mongol occupation in
the second part of the thirteenth century is very great. The latter are far
simpler in all respects: their ornamentation lacks sumptuous Byzantine
patterns, like enamelled flowers. Interlace and animal-motifs now fill the
leaves with imagination and fantasy.

The artistic expression of this period is most clearly exemplified by
illuminated manuscripts of Novgorod origin. More manuscripts have
survived from Novgorod than from any other Russian town or centre.
These Novgorod books include the Simon (or George Lotysh) Lectionary

vi The Simon Psalter

of 1270 (Pl. 11), a Psalter from the Khludov collection (vi–vii, Pls. 12–15), the Solovetsky Liturgy (viii) and the Liturgy of St Antony of Rome, which dates from the early fourteenth century but contains a miniature whose style shows little development from that of the late thirteenth century (ix).

Novgorodian miniatures of the latter part of the thirteenth century are by no means all of equal quality, but all are alike in their treatment of figures and manner of painting. They combine a richness of spiritual content with simplicity of means of representation, and in this they are characteristic of all Russian painting in the late thirteenth century. The style is well represented by the portrayals of the Evangelists in the Simon Lectionary (Pl. 11). The large figures of the Evangelists are majestic and monumental, their faces tense and frozen. Spiritual strength seems to distance them from the associations of everyday life. At the same time, the illuminator makes use of the bright colours and the ornamental, flat type of representation so beloved of the common people. The colour is clear, without gradations, and simple. The contrast of the bright, pure reds and greens has a naive freshness. There is no interest in modelling, the linear is stressed throughout, in both the outlines of the figures and the depiction of the robes. The inner tension of the images is conveyed almost entirely by expressiveness of drawing. The painting appears to play no part in this;

indeed it seems even to be used to reduce the tension by its simplicity and brightness. Only in the latter part of the thirteenth century, when Russia was largely isolated from the Byzantine world, did her artists create icons that are both majestic and simplified.

Fewer manuscripts have been preserved from other areas of Russia than from Novgorod, which was not invaded by the hordes of Batu Khan or devastated. Possibly fewer books were produced in the Russian lands overrun by the Mongols than in this relatively free north-Russian town. The surprising fact is, not that so few manuscripts of this period have survived, but that any survive at all – that books were copied, collected and read amid the universal devastation; that Russian culture did not disappear, or even decline, despite impoverishment and material destruction.

Among the manuscripts produced in Russia during the period of Mongol domination is a unique copy of the Chronicle of George Hamartolus, made in Tver (Pl. 17). There are also two manuscripts from Galich-Volynian Russia: the Homilies of St Gregory the Great (Pl. 16) and the Homilies of St Ephraem of Syria (x). They share a common imagery and style. Both have simple, colourful painting, and an intense spirituality.

A considerably greater number of illuminated manuscripts survive from the fourteenth than from the thirteenth century, and those of the later period are more varied and complex. This diversity is to be explained by the fact that Russian art, including that of the miniature, which had been partially isolated from Byzantine art in the thirteenth century, now re-established its contacts. The art of the miniature reflects the many connections of Russian art with Byzantium and the Balkans no less strongly than the fresco and the icon of the period.

The majority of fourteenth-century illuminated manuscripts belong to the second half of the century. The style of the few surviving early fourteenth-century miniatures reveals a combination of interest in earlier traditions and innovations from the art of the Byzantine world. The stylistic renewal of Russian painting was slow and gradual, like the re-awakening of the whole of the life of the country, still under Mongol control but showing increasing independence. The austere, harsh artistic idiom of the thirteenth century was modified towards a greater flexibility. However, fresh possibilities of expression were not discovered all at once.

A representative miniature of this period is The Mission of the Apostles in the Siya Lectionary of 1340, produced in Moscow under Ivan I Kalita (Pl. 20). Christ and the Apostles are very alike in appearance and expression – a single thought is impressed, as it were, on a multitude of faces. This repetitiveness is a characteristic of an archaic style, and had been general in Russian painting of the thirteenth century. The composition indicates no ground-level, nor is there any other horizontal supporting line: the weighty figures are set in an abstract, two-dimensional space. The atmosphere of the scene is aloof, lacking any sense of involvement. This type of rendering and air of detachment, as well as the manner of painting the faces with an expressive outline and thin, even layer of light-coloured paint, were all characteristic features of the thirteenth-century Russian miniature. However, this leaf also displays stylistic features that are far freer and more pictorial, and characteristic of the fourteenth century. The colours are bright, with an abundance of light blues, golden yellows and emerald greens. The soft folds of the robes are conveyed through subtle gradations of shade, rather than by sharp, conventional highlights. The multitude of broken tones and contrasts, and the transparency of the colours, give the painting depth and brilliance. There is great gentleness and vitality in this miniature, achieved by the same stylistic means as those employed by Byzantine art in the period.

A combination of the older artistic conventions and fourteenth-century features is found also in the miniatures of the Theodore Lectionary (Pls. 18– 19). This book was probably produced in Moscow, or might have originated in Rostov or Yaroslavl. The scribes and painters who created it were obviously imitating the splendid Russian manuscripts of the pre-Mongolian period. The solemnity and sumptuousness of the representations are reminiscent of the work of a much earlier period – the eleventh and twelfth centuries – and of the tastes of the princely house of Kiev. Volume is absent, there is no modelling, forms have lost their plasticity, and the completely flat figures seem to be hovering, surrounded by a faint radiance, their outlines rimmed with gold. The rare, precious colours glitter like enamels. The whole depiction is dematerialized, divorced from the familiar and earthly, transfigured, and emanates a deep sense of spirituality. These qualities, archaic for the fourteenth century, are interestingly combined with features of contemporary Byzantine painting, with which the illuminator must have been familiar: hence, again, the gentleness and vitality in

vii The Simon Psalter

place of a hieratic monumentality. Theodore's type of face, with its small features and air almost of intimacy, is far removed from the austere Russian images of the thirteenth century. There is a new pictorial quality in the modelling of the faces. No established new style can be claimed for these miniatures, yet it is obvious that the convention has somehow changed, and that new elements, similar to those that renewed Byzantine art after the re-occupation of Constantinople in 1261, have entered Russian art of the early fourteenth century.

There was little development in Russian art during the period from the early to mid-fourteenth century: we find the same lack of unity of style, the same attachment to tradition combined with a search for stylistic renewal. Russian contacts with Byzantine art were increasingly numerous: according to the Russian chronicles, Greek artists were working in both Moscow and Novgorod during the 1330s and 1340s. The miniatures of the Lectionary from the Khludov collection, produced in Novgorod around the middle of the fourteenth century, give a clear idea of tastes of this period (xi, Pl. 22). The composition is no longer conventional and static; instead there are developed settings, and objects have perspective and modelling. The search for three dimensions has led to naive exaggeration: the figures appear excessively large, the robes over-sumptuous and their folds too

viii The Solovetsky
Liturgy

heavy and abundant. Modelling and foreshortening are so far emphasized
that the illuminator evidently attached special value to them. True, the air of
constraint has not yet vanished from the style of these miniatures, but in
general, an obvious imitation of fourteenth-century Byzantine models
produces a style more flexible and richer in variety than that of thirteenth-
century Russian art.

The miniatures of the second half of the fourteenth century and the early
fifteenth century are both rich and varied, and are often equal in quality to
the frescoes and icons of the period. Alongside the illuminated manuscripts
of the important cities, Novgorod and Moscow, others have survived from
local centres – Smolensk, Ryazan, Pskov, Vladimir, Suzdal, Galich
(Kostroma area) and Yaroslavl. The miniatures from these places are extremely diverse stylistically. The artistic life of this period was marked by
exploration, and from among the multitude of possibilities, the choice that
would eventually bring the impress of a national style to Russian art had
not yet been made. Respect for tradition was combined with an interest in
innovations from the art of the whole Orthodox Christian world.

The miniatures of a number of manuscripts around the turn of the
fourteenth century, from both Novgorod and Moscow, are in a late
fourteenth-century Byzantine style associated in Russia with the name of

the great painter Theophanes the Greek. The details of the latter's career are known from a letter written by a Russian admirer of his paintings named Epifaniy the Wise, in about 1415. He was one of several talented Greek artists who left Constantinople in search of work during the civil wars of the mid-fourteenth century. He apparently painted frescoes in a considerable number of churches in Constantinople, and in Russian cities including Novgorod and Moscow. He was also famous for his expertise in icon painting and manuscript illumination. Epifaniy notes his professionalism and fluency, in contrast to those Russian painters who always needed some model in front of them to copy.

It is unlikely, however, that any of the illuminators who worked on these manuscripts imitated Theophanes directly. More probably they had come into contact in one way or another with the circles of artists, evidently quite extensive in Russia, for whom the work of Theophanes was a model. It is also possible that other Greek masters who were working in Russia in the same expressive and intense manner as Theophanes the Greek may have been a source of knowledge and inspiration – the painters of the frescoes in the Church of the Dormition at Volotovo, near Novgorod, for example.

Among illuminated manuscripts of this kind are the so-called Psalter of

xi Lectionary

xii Lectionary

Ivan the Terrible (Pl. 26), produced in Novgorod in the last third of the fourteenth century, and the late fourteenth-century Lectionary of the Chudov monastery (Pl. 27), which like The Ladder to Paradise of St John Climacus (xiv, Pl. 42) of the first third of the fifteenth century, from the Desnitsky collection, was written and illuminated in Moscow. The most splendid of these manuscripts is the Psalter of Ivan the Terrible, which belonged to Ivan IV in the sixteenth century, and was presented by him to the Trinity Monastery of St Sergius. The large book with fine script is adorned with a multitude of interlace and animal-motif headpieces and initials. It also contains two miniatures of King David and the Temple Musician Asaph. The figures are shown inside a church, depicted flat and as if in section, the interior covered with ornament of knots, fantastic monsters and grotesque representations of people. This ornament is executed with calligraphic refinement. The figures are painted confidently, but lightly. The illuminator is fond of asymmetry, which adds tension to the figures. This device was widespread also in Late Byzantine painting. The illuminator of these Novgorodian miniatures introduces a characteristic irregularity into the faces: the softness of the highlighting creates the illusion of shifting patches of light. The painted surface, of light blues and browns, is full of light, and almost appears to quiver. These rapid, precise effects of the painting recall the frescoes in the Church of the Dormition at Volotovo, where the figures are similar in type to those in the Novgorodian manuscript miniatures.

Some Russian illuminated manuscripts of the late fourteenth and early fifteenth centuries can be linked with other Byzantine and Balkan sources. Russia's contacts with the area were fairly wide: we know of icons brought to Russia from Constantinople, and of Russian translations of Greek, Bulgarian and Serbian manuscripts. We know, also, the names of Greek masters who worked in Russia, and of frescoes painted in Russian towns by Greek and southern Slav masters. Consequently Russian painters had available to them a variety of Greek and Serbian models. These foreign masters were imitated by Russian miniaturists, and in some cases their works were directly copied – although always adapted in the 'Russian manner'. Among the obvious copies are the illustrations for a Psalter of 1397 (Pls. 28–9), written by Spiridon in Kiev but illuminated in Moscow. The numerous small miniatures scattered in the manuscript's margins are copied with scrupulous care and great calligraphic skill. In their drawing and composition they resemble the illuminations of Byzantine psalters of the latter part of the eleventh century (particularly that in the British Library, Add. ms 19352, known as the Psalter of Theodore and painted in 1066). One of these probably served as a model for the artist working in Moscow during the late fourteenth century. Apart from adopting the iconography, he borrowed from the eleventh century the ethereal quality of the figures, a light refinement of style, and the iridescent colours that glitter beneath a network of fine golden lines.

These miniatures nevertheless belong to the art of the late fourteenth century. For all the imitation of older models, they are the products of their age. The spiritual climate of the period has introduced an inner tension, resulting in faces that are expressively asymmetrical, colourful drawing that is sharp and often dynamic, and colour-modelling of form that is rapid and light. The stylistic techniques here are the same as those of the miniatures of the Psalter of Ivan IV the Terrible and the Volotovo frescoes, and the illuminations of a number of Greek manuscripts of the middle and later fourteenth century. This style was one of many adopted in Byzantine painting in the later fourteenth century. In some of its qualities it resembles, too, the art of Theophanes the Greek; or at least, it is a product of the artistic climate of that period. If there is no more than a hint of this style in the miniatures of the Psalter, it is enough to transform and heighten the eleventh-century prototype.

The miniature of Christ in Majesty (Pl. 30) from a Gospel produced *c.* 1400 in Pereyaslavl-Zalessky, near Moscow, relates to a different area of iconographic and stylistic influence, in that it reflects the spiritual attitudes of the time. The expression of the face of Christ is restrained, with no emotion, no exaggerated spirituality. On the contrary, there is total outward calm, a quiet inner absorption, an atmosphere of silence and prayerful concentration. The inward gaze is intent and radiant. The lively, spontaneous pictorial quality and the fluidity of the paint-layers of the other manuscripts described are entirely absent here, for they are considered unsuitable for the creation of an image of spiritual contemplation. The painting is also restrained – no bright colours, no heavy strokes. The brown flesh-tone of the face merges into green shades; the paint does not model or create depth, but serves merely as a kind of covering. Purely pictorial devices must not distract the viewer from contemplating the spiritual depths of the image. The only emphasis in the painting of the face is the intense white light that falls upon it; in comparison, all the tones seem inert. The light on Christ's cloak is equally significant; the golden rays falling on the fabric create a dense radiance. A heightened attention to the symbolism of divine light, capable of purifying and transfiguring the flesh, was characteristic of the spiritual concerns of the age, and, consequently, of Orthodox art of the latter part of the fourteenth century. This was the period of the triumph of the teaching of St Gregory Palamas, who promoted the theory and practice of Hesychasm, a new kind of mystical monasticism. The miniature of Christ in Majesty (like the icon of Christ Pantocrator of 1363 in the Hermitage Museum, Leningrad, and the miniatures in the theological works of John VI Cantacuzenus, Bibliothèque nationale, Paris, Gr. 1242) well represents the ideas of the adherents of this new spiritual movement.

Russian manuscripts of the latter part of the fourteenth century sometimes contain miniatures similar in style to Serbian illuminations. Indeed, the resemblance is so strong that one cannot help wondering whether these pictures were created by Russian artists imitating Serbian models, or by Serbian artists living in Russia. We know that in this period artists moved

xiii Archbishop's
Liturgy

round the Orthodox world freely, receiving commissions in the various countries. The Orthodox Christian world was international in both the religious and the artistic sense. Yet this age coincided with a period of national revival in Russia, and of Russian creativity in towns and monasteries. Many churches received frescoes, icons were painted everywhere, and artists were in great demand. Greek and Balkan painters were readily accepted in Russia, and even Russian manuscripts offer evidence of their presence. Russian literature, language, palaeography and illuminated manuscripts all came under what is known as 'the second South Slav influence'. Examples of this are the miniatures of a Novgorodian Lectionary of the last third of the fourteenth century, in the collection of the Historical Museum, Moscow (Pl. 31). The iconography is unusual, and in Russian art, unfamiliar: the Evangelists are depicted standing holding scrolls, like Prophets. Their figures are strong and well-proportioned, and modelled to the extent that they resemble statues. At the same time, their bent poses seem mannered. The broad faces with their high cheekbones and large straight noses are very life-like. Nowhere is the skin coloured in broad areas; its different shades create a completely iridescent surface. The colours are applied on the parchment as distinct strokes. In all respects these miniatures are remote from Novgorodian art. Their closest models

xiv The Ladder
to Paradise
of St John Climacus

are found in Serbian art of the late fourteenth century, for example in the frescoes in the Church of St Andrew on the River Treska, or the Deesis icons from the Monastery of Chilandarion Athos. Such Balkan art of the late fourteenth century stimulated images of a monumental type, which developed the style of the late thirteenth century known from the frescoes in the Church of the Virgin of Perivleptos in Ohrid, and the icon of St Matthew, also in Ohrid.

Yet the power of art of around 1300 was not to be recaptured, and despite a borrowed monumentalism, the images of the later fourteenth century are marked by mannerism. This development is peculiar to the art of the late fourteenth century, arising from a complex interaction between artistic exploration and conservatism. Balkan painting is strangely echoed in the miniatures of the Novgorodian manuscript. It is interesting that the only works of art in Russia that resemble these miniatures are the frescoes of the church at Kovalevo near Novgorod, which we know to be the work of Serbian artists. Even so, the similarity between the two is not exact, by any means; there are no completely identical images in the Kovalevo frescoes. Their common feature is the non-Russian, Balkan nature of their style.

The most intensive artistic activity in Russia in the fourteenth and early fifteenth centuries took place in Moscow and Novgorod. It was here that

xv St Basil the Great's
Sermon on Lent

artists from other Orthodox countries gathered, and that splendid manuscripts were created, with miniatures that reflected the wide variety of styles of Late Byzantine and Balkan art. They include a Liturgy from Novgorod of about 1400 (xiii), a Moscow Gospels of 1401 (Pl. 33), a Moscow Gospels of the early fifteenth century (Pl. 34), a Moscow Lectionary of the late fourteenth century (Pl. 35), a Moscow Acts of the Apostles of the first third of the fifteenth century (Pl. 40), and a Moscow Gospels of the last third of the fifteenth century with the miniatures of the first half of the fifteenth century (Pl. 41). All the miniatures range with contemporary Byzantine art in conception, style and quality – provincialism and archaism are absent. There is more stylistic diversity to be found among them than unity of aims and tastes.

This unity only really began to develop at the beginning of the fifteenth century, during the period when the great artist Andrei Rublev was working, when the features of the Moscow style, which was gradually to become the national style, were being recognized and perfected. Among illuminated manuscripts, these stylistic features are seen most clearly in the miniatures of the famous Moscow Khitrovo Lectionary, which shows the Evangelists with their symbols (Pls. 36–9). They may, indeed, be the work of Andrei Rublev himself. The splendid leaves are remarkable for their

xvi The Khitrovo
Lectionary

abundance of light, the radiance of their colours and the interplay of light blue, lilac and golden-yellow. They are very different from the depictions in fourteenth-century manuscripts – the facial types have become softer, with a smooth, rounded contour and small features; the colours are paler and more radiant, and the colouring is of greater importance. In the painting of the faces, use is made of broad green shadows which give them a touch of softness, even benevolence. There is a new fondness for rounded, unbroken contours and areas of solid colour, a rejection of traditional highlights, and the use of lighter, less conspicuous modelling for the robes.

During the fifteenth century, Russian art tended increasingly towards uniformity of style, and this trend was reflected in the Russian miniature. The style that developed in Moscow at the beginning of the century, described above, became, in the centralized State, a national Russian style. Paper progressively displaced parchment, and this influenced painting, for thick, smooth, glossy parchment offers a different kind of surface from that of thin paper. The layer of paint became more delicate. The proportions of the pages changed, their arrangement becoming more compact, less majestic and sumptuous. The broad margins disappeared, and the script became closer. The images began to evince warmth and intimacy.

A considerable number of fifteenth-century illuminated manuscripts

xvii The Four Gospels

xviii The Acts
of the Apostles

have survived. Most belong to the last third of the century; for the most part they were produced in Moscow and neighbouring monasteries. Fine and characteristic examples are a Lectionary of the mid-fifteenth century (Pl. 43), a Gospels of the last third of the fifteenth century (Pl. 44), and a Book of the Prophets of 1489 (Pl. 45). However, illuminations painted far away from Moscow show the same stylistic features, as in a Gospel of south Russian origin from the Rumiantsev collection, and the single miniature from the Biblical Miscellany of the Undolsky collection (Pl. 46), the provenance of which is unknown.

The depictions of the figures in Russian miniatures are no longer based strictly on Byzantine models. Russian artists have developed new conventions, intended to create an effect of spiritual warmth. The figures are drawn with smooth curves. The robes are painted without highlights, their draping indicated by short, light lines of colour that are less obtrusive than long, vertical highlights. The robes seem to billow out, as if filled with air. The cloaks do not wrap the figures tightly, but envelop them loosely, giving a light and airy appearance. The favourite colour-ranges are light, eschewing contrasts, with soft shades and gentle tonal gradations of pale half-tints. The radiant colour-combinations, often light blues and golden ochres, emanate quiet concentration. The restraint of the colouring creates

xix The Morozov
Lectionary

an impression, not of an external source of light, but of a radiance from
within that spiritualizes form and matter. The elongated proportions of the
figures make them seem almost to be hovering. The smooth outlines of the
heads, the Russian types of face and the expressions – often of reconcilia-
tion, forgiveness and loving-kindness – are drawn from the art of Andrei
Rublev. The painting of the faces is based on barely perceptible intermingling of shades of brown and green. The smoothness of the paint makes
the painting itself almost unnoticeable. All these features are in line with
the general trend of the art of this period, which was towards lyricism, and
an atmosphere of prayer and contemplation.

In fifteenth-century miniatures the architectural backgrounds are no
longer in balance with the overall composition. They no longer serve to
organize space; instead they have a purely decorative function. Forms lack
weight and volume; they are flat and evenly coloured, and their proportions lack realism. Such architectural backgrounds have been transferred to
the miniature from fifteenth-century icon painting, where they did originally have a function: to punctuate the physical structure of the high icon-
screen which separated the sanctuary from the nave of the church.

The style of Russian fifteenth-century miniatures creates a particular
emotional impression. The smooth lines, the harmony of the colour-range,

xx Book of St John
Damascene

xxi Bible

the melting softness of the paint and the kindly facial expressions all convey a sense of warmth and intimacy that is characteristic of almost all Russian art of the period. Like icons, Russian miniatures reflected a spiritual climate to be found especially in the monasteries that had developed under the influence of the teaching of St Sergius of Radonezh and St Nilus of Sora – a climate of patriarchal ideas concerning spiritual brotherhood and moral perfectibility, in their simplicity and idealism similar to the ideas of the Christian community of the early centuries after Christ.

At the same time, certain characteristics of the style, such as the closed contours, the radiance of colours, the smoothness of the faces, and the outward restraint and lack of concrete associations that might distract from spiritual concentration, are in keeping with the calm contemplativeness of the Orthodox mind.

The painting of the fifteenth century is one of the key stages in the development of Russian art: a period of the flowering of a truly national Russian style, independent of the art of the rest of the Orthodox world. The miniatures executed in this style possess great artistic merit, second only in perfection to fifteenth-century Russian icon painting.

The last third of the fifteenth century marked both the peak of the development of the Russian national style and the onset of its decline.

Already by the end of the fifteenth and beginning of the sixteenth century, manuscript illumination was losing its inner symbolic meaning, and a certain aridity appeared. Alongside images full of spiritual warmth, there are miniatures that point to the beginnings of the decline of this style, such as those of the Gospels of 1507 created by Theodosios, the son of the famous artist Dionisy (Pl. 48). Theodosios' miniatures are outwardly brilliant and full of a refined elegance, but they are overloaded with detail. The gentle humanity characteristic of fifteenth-century works has been replaced by a superficial prettiness. The extreme refinement and richness of ornament have cost dear. In general, it may be said that from the sixteenth century onward, the art of the miniature took on a more external aspect. It developed a literary flavour, a preoccupation with subjects and details. The close of the fifteenth century was a turning point.

xiv The Ladder to Paradise
of St John Climacus (cf. Pl. 42)
St John Climacus' Homilies, f. 1v
Moscow, first third of 15th century

xv St Basil the Great's
Sermon on Lent
St Basil the Great, f. 1v
Moscow, the Chudov Monastery
(written by the monk Antony), 1388
Parchment 30.4×22.5 cm (11⅞×8¾ in.)
Historical Museum, Moscow,
collection of the Chudov
Monastery (ms 10)

xvi The Khitrovo Lectionary
(cf. Pls. 36–9)
St Matthew, f. 44v. Detail (*see Pl. 36*)
Moscow, late 14th or early
15th century

xvii The Four Gospels
St Matthew, f. 10v
Moscow (?), late 15th century
Paper 19.5×12.5 cm (7⅝×4⅞ in.)
Saltykov-Shchedrin Public Library,
Leningrad (ms Q1 14)

xviii The Acts of the Apostles
The Apostle Peter, f. 97v
Moscow, last third of 15th century
Paper 30.5×20.5 cm (12×8 in.)
Lenin Library, Moscow,
collection of the Moscow
Theological Academy (ms 4)

xix The Morozov Lectionary
St Luke, f. 130v
Moscow, early 15th century
Parchment 35.7×29 cm (14×11⅜ in.)
Armoury, Moscow (ms 11056)

xx Book of St John Damascene
*Allegory of the Months
(August and September)*, f. 268v
Moscow, late 15th century
Paper 20.2×14 cm (8⅞×5½ in.)
Lenin Library, Moscow,
collection of the Trinity
Monastery of St Sergius (ms 177)

xxi Bible
*Scenes from the Life of
King David*, f. 173v
1507
Paper 30.5×21 cm (12×8¼ in.)
The USSR Academy of Sciences,
Leningrad (ms 24.4.28)

Plates and Commentaries

1 The Ostromir Lectionary
St John and St Prochoros, f. 1v

Saltykov-Shchedrin Public Library, Leningrad,
ms Fn I. 5
Kiev, 1056–7
Parchment 35×30 cm (13¾×11¾ in.); miniature
24×20 cm (9⅜×7⅞ in.)*
294 ff., 3 miniatures

PROVENANCE

*Until 17th century, Novgorod; 1650s (during the
reforms of Patriarch Nikon) Moscow; early 18th
century, Church of the Resurrection in the Moscow
Kremlin; 1720 St Petersburg; 1806 Public Library,
St Petersburg*

The Ostromir Lectionary, the earliest dated Russian manuscript, was created
in Kiev for Ostromir, Governor of Novgorod and relative of the Kievan prince
Iziaslav Yaroslavich. Written on fine parchment, it is an example of the type of
book that could have been commissioned by a prince for use as an expensive
gift. The manuscript was embellished with four portrait-miniatures of the
Evangelists (three survived) and a wealth of ornament.

St John is depicted with his disciple St Prochoros, who is recording the
divine revelations and visions of his teacher. This scene is enclosed by a
quatrefoil frame with an ornamental border and a large enamel-like flower in
each corner. The composition is in the form of a cross, with the vertical axis
formed by the figure of St John with his hands raised in prayer and an eagle
swooping down towards him (the eagle was the traditional sign of St John). The
horizontal axis is formed by the two petals of the quatrefoil, with St Prochoros
on the left and a chair, table and lectern on the right.

---

* Measurements are given in centimetres and inches, height preceding width. Where miniatures
are not surrounded by a border their dimensions are not separately indicated.

2 The Ostromir Lectionary
St Luke, f. 87v

Saltykov-Shchedrin Public Library, Leningrad,
ms Fn I. 5
Kiev, 1056–7
Parchment 35×30 cm (13¾×11¾ in.); miniature
25×19 cm (9¾×7⅜ in.)
294 ff., 3 miniatures

The miniature portraying St Luke is set in a rectangular frame and surrounded by a wide ornamental border, as was frequent with Byzantine miniatures. St Luke is depicted standing stiffly posed in a room which contains a seat, desk and writing implements, gazing intently towards the heavenly vision and raising his hands in prayer. The Holy Spirit appears from heaven as a winged ox bearing a scroll, the sign of St Luke.

The representation of the figure is different in style in this and the preceding miniature (Pl. 1), and they are undoubtedly by different artists. The Saint's robes are covered with a fine web of gold lines, as if to represent divine light; the shape of the figure and its colours are almost lost to view beneath the bright golden mesh. The figure becomes ethereal, seeming almost ready to ascend to heaven. This type of representation recalls the visions described by the Byzantine mystic Simeon the New Theologian, and recurs constantly in Byzantine miniatures in the late tenth century, and throughout the following century. However, in the Kievan miniature the gold mesh of St Luke's robes evokes the technique of cloisonné enamel. The Saint's face, hands and feet, too, are depicted in a manner strongly reminiscent of enamel, a popular medium in Kiev.

Whereas in Byzantine art the method of conveying light by fine gold lines was used sparingly and in conjunction with other representational devices, with Kievan craftsmen it became the chief means of creating symbolic imagery in an exalted style.

3 The Mstislav Lectionary
St John and St Prochoros, f. 1

Historical Museum, Moscow (transferred from the
Synodal Collection), ms 1203
Novgorod, early 12th century
Parchment 35.3×28.6 cm (13⅞×11¼ in.); miniature
20.5×20 cm (8×7¾ in.)
213 ff., 4 miniatures

PROVENANCE

*Patriarchal Vestry; 1917 transferred to the Synodal
(Patriarchal) Library, Moscow; 1920 Historical
Museum, Moscow*

This manuscript was written under the patronage of Prince Mstislav of
Novgorod by the scribe Alexa Lazarevich, who records that he is the son of a
priest. It is noted for its high quality, and, like the Ostromir Lectionary, is the
type of book found in a Russian prince's home. The sumptuous cover is of
silver-gilt, with enamelling and precious stones, and was specially commissioned in Constantinople.

It is highly probable that the illuminator of this Lectionary was imitating the
Ostromir Lectionary, for the general appearance and the miniatures of the
Novgorod manuscript follow the Kievan book closely. But it is even more
probable that both manuscripts had a common prototype. The miniature
portraying St John is an almost exact repetition of St John from the Ostromir
Lectionary (Pl. 1) in its composition, the quatrefoil bordering, the Byzantine
style of decoration and iconographical detail. Even the Saint's pose and the
impassioned expression of his face turned towards the heavenly vision, are alike
in the two miniatures. The only missing element is the lion, which in the
Ostromir Lectionary strides across the top of the vignette.

The figures, the folds of their garments, and the distribution of light and
shade also show a striking resemblance to the Ostromir Lectionary. The
master's acquaintance with the Byzantine tradition can be detected in the
harmony of proportion, the plasticity and the pictorial expressiveness of the
Novgorod miniature.

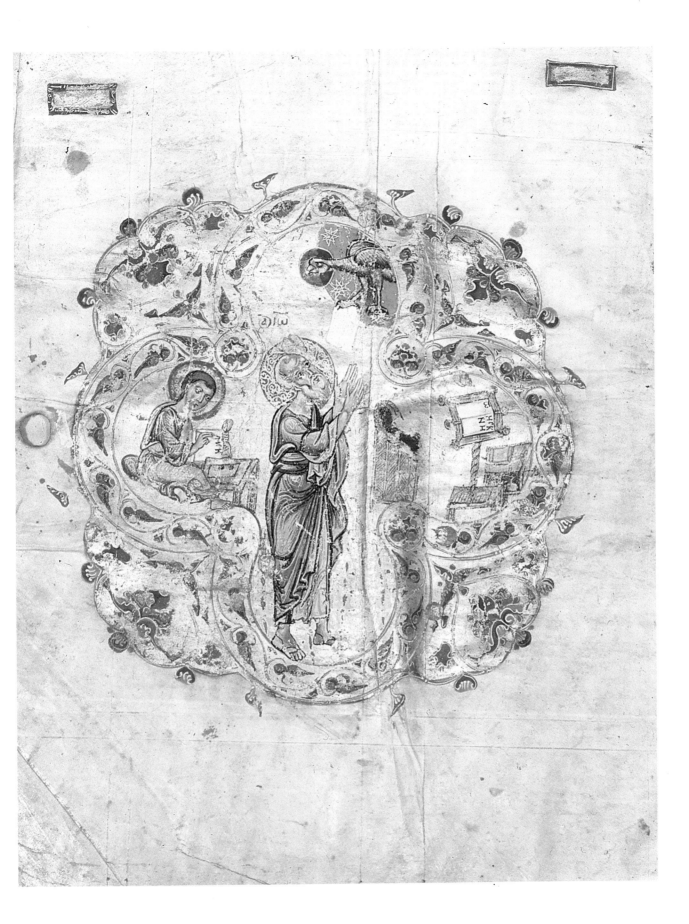

4 The Mstislav Lectionary
St Luke, f. 69v

Historical Museum, Moscow (transferred from the
Synodal Collection), ms 1203
Novgorod, early 12th century
Parchment 35.3×28.6 cm (13⅞×11¼ in.); miniature
26×25.5 cm (10⅛×10 in.)
213 ff., 4 miniatures

This miniature, like the preceding one, is similar in composition and iconography to the depiction in the Ostromir Lectionary (Pl. 2). It has also the same inscription: 'The Holy Ghost appears to St Luke in the shape of an ox'. There is, however, a difference in imagery and style. The Novgorod folio is also magnificently decorated and lavishly ornamented with gold, yet here the attention of the spectator is directed to the spiritual message of the image. Enormous intensity is conveyed by the Saint's exalted gaze, his imploring gesture, and his large figure that seems to strain out towards the spectator.

The picture recalls monumental paintings. Compared to Kievan miniatures, the lines here are heavier and more imperative, the colours are brighter and more strongly contrasting, and the whole manner is broader and more painterly. Novgorod miniatures have a greater intensity and expressiveness. This is a reflection of both local tastes and the advent with the twelfth century of a new stylistic epoch, bringing an increase of energy and movement to Byzantine art.

5 The Mstislav Lectionary
St Mark, f. 123v

Historical Museum, Moscow (transferred from the
Synodal Collection), ms 1203
Novgorod, early 12th century
Parchment 35.3×28.6 cm (13⅞×11¼ in.); miniature
24.4×18.4 cm (9½×7⅜ in.)
213 ff., 4 miniatures

The composition of this page repeats that of St John from the Ostromir
Lectionary (Pl. 1). The quatrefoil design containing the scene has rectangular
corners set between the petals, the lower pair forming two platforms: the
Saint's chair is placed on one, his table and lectern on the other. The figure of St
Mark stands out prominently against the light-coloured, patterned background. A heavily decorated, Byzantine-style rectangular border surrounds
the quatrefoil design. The fine, lattice-like tracery behind the Saint shines like a
lighted window, giving an impression of airiness. Again, the representation is
almost identical to that from the Ostromir Lectionary, while the general effect
is different. The body of the Saint seems foreshortened, out of proportion to
the head. Emphasis is placed on expressive drawing; the colouring is bright and
uniform, without gradations. This type of painting does not display the subtle
harmony of Byzantine art, but offers instead a pleasing freshness and dynamism. The monumental quality, the heightened expressiveness, the intense
spirituality and the dramatic impact – these are the features of the new style,
which had already evolved in Novgorod by the beginning of the twelfth
century and continued to flourish throughout its course, though undergoing a
certain degree of change.

6 The Sviatoslav Codex

*The Fathers of the Church and Monks,
Authors of the Texts*, f. 128v

Historical Museum, Moscow (transferred from the
Synodal Collection), ms 31-д
Kiev, 1073
Parchment 33.5×25.5 cm (13⅛×10 in.)
266 ff., 6 miniatures (2 ff. with signs of the Zodiac in
margins)

PROVENANCE

*Novgorod; 1650s probably brought by the Patriarch
Nikon to the Monastery of the Resurrection in New
Jerusalem near Moscow; 1834 Synodal (Patriarchal)
Library, Moscow; 1920 Historical Museum, Moscow*

This manuscript, containing preachings on Christian ethics, passages of Roman
and Byzantine history and texts on logic and grammar, is a kind of medieval
encyclopaedia. The text was in all probability compiled in Preslav in the tenth
century, during the reign of Simeon. In 1073 it was copied in Kiev for Prince
Iziaslav Yaroslavich, and in the same year it fell into the hands of his brother
Sviatoslav who captured Kiev.

The copy made for Iziaslav was decorated with five miniatures, one of which
depicted Christ while the remaining four represented the Fathers of the
Church and the monks, authors of the book. These four miniatures are large,
decorative compositions with ornamentation typical of the art of Kiev. Each
miniature contains a conventional representation of a one- or three-domed
church building. Such representations also occur in Byzantine manuscripts,
particularly during the twelfth century.

The churches in such depictions are surrounded by birds, usually peacocks,
much favoured by Byzantine painters, and executed in Kievan manuscripts
with a typically Byzantine refinement. The Fathers of the Church are shown
standing within an arch, their figures tiny compared to the size of the ornament, but still impressive in their effect of austerity. With large heads and
severe expressions, and prominent, staring eyes suggesting religious fervour,
the Fathers personify asceticism and self-denial. This type of portrayal had
been known in Byzantium from the sixth century onwards.

This miniature is noteworthy for the ease with which the artist combines
elements from two opposed traditions: the highly refined, aristocratic art of
Constantinople, and the simpler and cruder depictions characteristic of ascetic
Eastern Christendom. Kiev was open to influences from each of these direc-
tions.

7 The Acts of the Apostles
The Apostles Peter and Paul, f. 1v

Historical Museum, Moscow (transferred from
the Synodal Collection), ms 7
Rostov the Great, 1220
Parchment 44.5×31.7 cm (17½×12⅜ in.);
miniature 35×22.5 cm (13¾×8¾ in.)
241 ff., 1 miniature

PROVENANCE

*1661 donated by the Patriarch Nikon to the
Monastery of the Resurrection in New Jerusalem
near Moscow; 1675 Patriarchal Vestry; 1920
Historical Museum, Moscow*

This large-scale, magnificent manuscript was produced under the patronage of
Cyril I, Bishop of Rostov, and was kept in his library which, according to the
chronicle, was very extensive. The single miniature it contains shows the
Apostles Peter and Paul, and is placed at the beginning of the book. In the
upper part of the arch, Christ, depicted in the celestial sphere, gives martyr's
crowns to the Apostles. The Apostles stand facing each other with their arms
raised in an attitude of worship, as if in silent communion.

The bright colouring of the miniature is achieved by a combination of pure
blues in the background and equally pure red in the arch. The rhythm of the
verticals, the gleaming colours, and elegant, elongated figures all recall Byzantine miniatures of the turn of the eleventh century, spiritualized and refined.
One such illuminated Greek manuscript (probably the Homilies of St Gregory
of Nazianzus, now in the Bodleian Library, Oxford, ms. Canon, Gr. 103) may
also have been in Cyril I's library, and provided a model for the Russian
copyist more than a century later.

8 Liturgy of St Barlaam of Khutyn

St John Chrysostom, f. 10v

Historical Museum, Moscow (transferred
from the Synodal Collection), ms 604
Galich-Volynian Principality,
late 12th or early 13th century
Parchment 24.5×19.5 cm (9⅝×7⅝ in.);
miniature 19×14 cm (7⅜×5½ in.)
29 ff., 2 miniatures

PROVENANCE

*1652 entered the Synodal (Patriarchal) Library
when Nikon was made Patriarch of Moscow; 1920
Historical Museum, Moscow*

The name of this Liturgy comes from a seventeenth-century record stating that
the book once belonged to St Barlaam, Abbot of the Khutyn Monastery in
Novgorod (late twelfth century). Certain linguistic and palaeographical fea-
tures indicate, however, that the manuscript was copied in south-western
Russia, in the principality of Galich-Volynia, at the turn of the twelfth century.
It contains two miniatures, depicting St Basil the Great and St John
Chrysostom. St John's oval face, with the high forehead of a philosopher, and
his thoughtful gaze, convey the impression of an intellect obedient to the spirit.
His elongated ascetic figure seems to float above the ground in the golden space
that symbolizes divine light. The lines are simple and clear, the contours
precise and austere; they are matched by a subtle and expressive range of
transparent colours. The silent dignity of the Saint and the quiet harmony of
the style suggest a mood of profound contemplation.

The master who created this miniature was undoubtedly familiar with
Byzantine art of the late twelfth and early thirteenth centuries. Reminiscent of
the miniatures of this manuscript are the Bishops in the murals of the Church
of the Virgin at Studenica in Yugoslavia (1208–9), the icon of St Euthymios in
the Monastery of St Catherine on Sinai (late twelfth to early thirteenth century), and the icon of St Gregory the Miracle-Worker (second half of the
twelfth century) now in the Hermitage Museum in Leningrad.

9 Lectionary
St Luke, f. 91

Tretyakov Gallery, Moscow, ms K-5348
Galich-Volynian Principality, early 13th century
Parchment 16×11 cm (6¼×4¼ in.); miniature
14×9 cm (5½×3½ in.)
229 ff., 4 miniatures

PROVENANCE

*1649 acquired for the library of the Synodal Printing
House; 1917 Tretyakov Gallery*

This small manuscript was in all probability intended for personal use, perhaps in a princely house.

Though St Luke is shown seated, his figure is infused with such movement and his robes are depicted so nervously that he seems charged with energy. The abundant, intricate folds of the Saint's robes are illuminated by a harsh, intense light. The elaborate lines of the figure, draped in heavy robes, do not coincide with the natural outlines of the human body. The head and hands of the Saint are strongly modelled. St Luke is the only Evangelist of the four in this manuscript to be portrayed with his sign – a winged ox descending from heaven. The picture is filled with objects, and the composition is not unlike a stage-set.

Many stylistic traits link this miniature with Byzantine art of the late twelfth century, when the fashion arose for portraying figures and their settings with an exaggerated emphasis on movement. This style of rushing figures and distorted draperies enjoyed a great vogue, not only in Constantinople, but throughout the European world, and it is not surprising to find it reflected in a Russian manuscript. But the delicacy of late twelfth-century art has given way to the powerful plasticity characteristic of thirteenth-century Byzantine art. This manuscript resembles in many respects the Gospels of around 1230 in the Athens National Library (Gr. 118), although the latter is somewhat later, and more classical in appearance.

It is interesting to note that illuminations of the Galich-Volynian Principality are closer to those of Byzantium than similar examples from northern and central area of Russia. The miniatures from this manuscript occupy a place apart in Russian art.

10 The Toshinich or Pantoleon Lectionary
St Pantoleon and St Catherine, f. 224

Saltykov-Shchedrin Public Library, Leningrad
(transferred from St Sophia Cathedral collection,
Kiev), ms 1
Novgorod, late 12th or early 13th century
Parchment 33.5×26 cm (13⅛×10¼ in.); miniature
23×17.5 cm (9×6⅞ in.)
224 ff., 1 miniature

PROVENANCE
St Sophia Cathedral, Novgorod

Commissioned by a patron named Pantoleon and written by a scribe named Maximus Toshinich, a Novgorodian priest, this manuscript was kept in the library of the Cathedral of St Sophia in Novgorod. The last folio contains the single illumination showing the martyrs St Pantoleon and St Catherine.

St Pantoleon, patron of physicians, is represented with a box of medicines, while St Catherine holds a cross. Both are depicted frontally, in solemn poses, with their feet firmly planted close to the lower border of the frame. In their blue robes suffused with light, which is rendered by lines and spots of white, the Saints appear like two luminous pillars set against the bright red background.

The atmosphere is joyful. The Saints are portrayed at the moment of their spiritual victory and celestial glory. The state of bliss of St Pantoleon and St Catherine is conveyed in several ways, from the resonant colours and lively combinations of tones to the calm grandeur of the figures themselves, clad in their lavishly decorated robes that seem to radiate light.

Stylistically, this illumination is reminiscent of late twelfth-century Novgorod frescoes, for instance those in the Church of St George in Staraya Ladoga, the Church of the Annunciation in Arkazhi and the Church of Christ at Nereditsa. The robes are modelled almost solely by means of highlights, as in fresco-painting. The forms seem flat, and the light acquires a dynamism from the patterns of the geometrically shaped highlights.

Concentration on the symbolic meaning of divine light, a feature of Byzantine art of the late twelfth century, is as evident in this miniature as in the murals of Novgorod. The figures' emotional intensity, implying spiritual fervour and zeal, is conveyed mainly by the luminous rays falling on their robes.

224.

11 The Simon (George Lotysh) Lectionary
St Matthew, f. 25v

Lenin Library, Moscow (acquired with the
Rumiantsev collection, Φ 256), ms 105
Novgorod, 1270
Parchment 27.3×21.9 cm (10¾×8½ in.); miniature
23.5×17.5 cm (9¼×6⅞ in.)
167 ff., 4 miniatures

PROVENANCE

*Early 19th century, bought by K. Averin, a
merchant, in the town of Staritsa; later bought
through philologists A. Vostokov and K. Kalaidovich
by Count N. Rumiantsev, Chancellor of Russia;
1924 entered Lenin Library with the Rumiantsev
collection*

The artist who created this manuscript, who is named as George, was the son of
Lotysh, a priest in Novgorod. The book was commissioned by a monk from
the Monastery of St George, named Simon. It was evidently at the wish of
Simon that the first miniature of the manuscript, portraying St John, also
contains St Simon instead of St Prochoros who usually acts as the secretary.

The manuscript is a large codex with whole-page portraits of the Four
Evangelists, headpieces and initials with animal-motifs. There is a marked
difference between this book and the miniatures it contains, and the manuscripts of the pre-Mongolian period. The parchment is thicker; the script not
so neat; the layout of the pages, though decorative, is not strict; instead of the
refined ornamentation of the earlier manuscripts there is a simplicity and a lack
of pretentiousness.

Each of the Evangelists is depicted standing beneath a brightly ornamented
arch against an equally bright background. Their figures are well-proportioned
but somewhat short, and lacking in elegance owing to their excessively large
heads. The illuminator makes extensive use of contrasting colours, eschewing
gradations. His favourite combination of reds, yellows and greens provides a
feeling of simple joy and vitality. In indicating the modelling of the robes of the
Evangelists, the artist uses black hatching in preference to highlights. The
figures are depicted two-dimensionally, standing out in silhouette against the
background.

The artist is not inclined to make his Saints unapproachable, or to emphasize
their other-worldliness. The Saints' faces are no longer neutral, as was thought
proper to an idealized Byzantine type of saint. Each has an element of personality and an expression – austere in the case of St Luke and genial in the case of
St Matthew.

In general, the artist's mode of expression deviates from that of Byzantine art
with its traditions going back to Antiquity. It was in the latter half of the
thirteenth century, during the years of Mongol-Tartar rule, that Russian
painting departed from Byzantine models to develop a distinctive style.

12 The Simon Psalter

Three Scenes from the Life of David, f. 52v
(before Psalm 32)

Historical Museum, Moscow (acquired with the
Khludov collection), ms 3
Novgorod, late 13th century
Parchment 27.5×20 cm (10¾×7¾ in.)
291 ff., 119 miniatures (110 in the margins or text)

PROVENANCE

*1571 brought from Novgorod, probably by Ivan IV
the Terrible; 17th century, St Euthymios Monastery
in Suzdal; 19th century, acquired by a collector,
A. Khludov; after Khludov's death,
St Nicholas Monastery in Moscow; 1917 Historical
Museum, Moscow*

The book was produced in Novgorod towards 1300. Like the preceding manuscript, it was commissioned by Simon, a monk from the Monastery of St George, and includes a representation of Simon's patron saint (f. 248v). The two manuscripts, however, appear to be copied and illuminated by different artists.

Of the Psalter's 119 miniatures, the first three are full-page illuminations depicting, respectively, Christ appearing to the Holy Women in the garden (f. 1), David composing the Psalms, with King Solomon and musicians (f. 1v, see fig. vi), and David writing down the Psalms (f. 6v). The rest of the illuminations are much smaller, and are either placed in the margins or set within the text. Sometimes several miniatures are grouped together within one frame. Above or beside the illuminations are commentaries written in Church Slavonic.

Folio 52v, before Psalm 32, contains three scenes from the life of David, linked by the ornamental frame. The top miniature shows Samuel anointing David (1 Samuel 16:13), the miniature at bottom left has Saul seated on the throne, with David and armed men standing before him (1 Samuel 17:38). The inscription reads: '[Saul] gives armour to his warrior departing for battle'. The miniature at bottom right shows David playing the harp before Saul (1 Samuel 16:23).

САМ
ИЛГПО
ВЛАЗАЕ
ТЬДВДА
НАЦРЬ
СТВО

ДА
ЧЛ

ПРИНОСИТЬДАНЬСВОН
КЪБОРЦЕКНЛЬ ХОТАШЮ
НТИСАЦ ЧНАБРА
НЬ

СЫНЗОЛЪВЕЛ ВАНВЪ
ЦЛЬДХЪ ДВАЪ ЖЕСЕГОН
ГОНИТЬЕГЦ
СЛНЕЬГ

13 The Simon Psalter

Three Scenes from the Life of David,
f. 239v (before Psalm 119)

Historical Museum, Moscow (acquired with the
Khludov collection), ms 3
Novgorod, late 13th century
Parchment 27.5×20 cm (10¾×7¾ in.); miniature
22.1×13.8 cm (8⅝×5⅜ in.)
291 ff., 119 miniatures

Between Psalms 118 and 119 is placed a full-page illumination showing three
further scenes from the life of David. Two upper scenes appear like a frieze,
separated by a temple. The one on the left depicts David interceding with the
Lord, facing the temple, while the angel behind him is smiting the people of
Jerusalem with a sword (2 Samuel 24:17). The inscription reads: 'David, seeing
the angel smite the people, prays'. The miniature on the right shows Absalom
seated on the throne with a sword in his hand and a pair of soldiers at either
side. The inscription reads: 'Absalom has ascended the throne of his father,
David'. The lower part of the miniature represents a battle between the soldiers
of David and Absalom. On the right is Absalom caught in an oak-tree. Below is
Joab thrusting three darts through the heart of Absalom (2 Samuel 18:14). The
inscriptions read: 'King David fights Absalom' and 'Absalom slain'. On the
right side of the frame is written: 'And when he polled his head... he weighed
the hair of his head at two hundred shekels after the king's weight' (2 Samuel
14:26).

14 The Simon Psalter

The Deesis with St Simon the Zealot,
f. 248v

Historical Museum, Moscow (acquired with the
Khludov collection), ms 3
Novgorod, late 13th century
Parchment 27.5×20 cm (10¾×7¾ in.)
291 ff., 119 miniatures

A small miniature showing the Deesis contains, besides the figures of Christ
with the Virgin and John the Baptist, the Apostle Simon the Zealot, perhaps
again at the wish of the monk Simon who commissioned the manuscript. The
representation of Simon the Zealot differs from that of other figures in the
miniature: he does not stand on a separate pedestal and is set apart from the
main compositional group.

The faces of the figures depicted in the Deesis and in other small scenes in the
manuscript have large features, fixed and often affected expressions, and an
intent gaze. The figures are well-proportioned here, but often short and heavy
in other scenes. The colours are bright, the lines strong and energetic. The
expressiveness of the illuminations in this manuscript links them with the
miniatures of the 1270 Lectionary (Pl. 11) and various Novgorod icons of the
second half of the thirteenth century.

Compared to those of the 1270 Lectionary, the illuminations of the Psalter
are more varied and more closely connected with the Byzantine tradition; but
they are not so deeply rooted in popular tradition.

The text below the illustration begins with the Slavonic letter B (the first
letter of the Church Slavonic word for 'Almighty'); this initial is drawn with
complicated interlace and animal decoration, typical of Novgorod ornament of
the thirteenth and fourteenth centuries.

ПРИПАДАЮКЪПНИ ХОДАТАИЦА
ИНКЪСПОУСНИВЕБОУ · ѠРАДОУ
ИНПОДАТИКЪДНЬСОУДНЫН ·

ИМАТЬ :·

СЕДЬРЖИТЕЛЮВЫШНИНБЕ НИ
ЖНИИТВАРИСЪДЕТЕЛЮ · ПОСТА
ВИНИСЛНЦЕПАПРОСВЕЩЕНИЕ
ДНИ · ЛОУНОУЖЕНZВЕZДЫНА
ПРОСВЕЩЕНИЕНОЩИ · РЕКЫН
ГНИСТЬ ЛЫСЕТОУКЪСИИТИ · НЖЬ
ЖЕОСВЕТИ ѠИ ЛЮКЪШЕЕСРДЦЕНОЕ
НЕСКРОПОКЛАДНИ ДАПАГОЛЮИТОБОЮ ·

15 The Simon Psalter

Christ Appearing to the Holy Women, f. 1

Historical Museum, Moscow (acquired with the
Khludov collection), ms 3
Novgorod, late 13th century
Parchment 27.5×20 cm (10¾×7¾ in.); miniature
21×13.5 cm (8¼×5¼ in.)
291 ff., 119 miniatures

The Holy Women, Martha and Mary, kneel at Christ's feet. The inscription at the top of the miniature reads: 'Christ, raised from the dead, appears to the Holy Women', and that below: 'Martha and Mary, sisters of Lazarus'.

The miniature is pasted on to the first folio of the manuscript, the verso of which has a full-page depiction of David composing Psalms, King Solomon and a group of musicians. This latter miniature must have been originally intended to be the first in the Psalter, but then the miniature with Christ and the Holy Women was introduced to precede it. Now the Psalter opened with the image of the resurrected Christ, as the patron who commissioned it intended; so the miniature must have been painted separately and probably by another artist. It has, however, some features (e.g. the figures of the Holy Women) in common with other illuminations in the Psalter, and is generally in accordance with the manuscript's style. This gives reason to suppose that it was produced either at the same time – that is, in the late thirteenth century – or a few years later, in the early 1300s.

Compositionally, the miniature belongs to the well-known iconographic type known in Greek as *Chairete* (Rejoice).

The figure of Christ is elegant and well-proportioned, his pose is supple and dynamic, his eyes are vivid and expressive. The face recalls that of Christ from the fresco of *The Descent into Hell* in the Monastery of Chora in Constantinople, a Byzantine masterpiece of around the year 1320.

The fine, ample folds of the robes and the elegant outlines of the drapery link this miniature with Byzantine art of the early fourteenth century. While the decorative treatment of the trees and the conventional composition are archaic features characteristic of thirteenth-century Novgorodian art, and are similar in style to the other miniatures in the manuscript, it is clear nevertheless that the illuminator of this additional folio was well acquainted with contemporary developments in Byzantine painting.

16 Homilies of St Gregory the Great

*Christ with St Gregory the Great
and St Eustace*, f. 1v

Saltykov-Shchedrin Public Library, Leningrad
(acquired with the Pogodin collection), ms 70
Galich-Volynian Principality, 13th century
Parchment 30.5×25 cm (12×9¾ in.); miniature
27×20 cm (10⅝×7¾ in.)
328 ff., 1 miniature

PROVENANCE

*Collection of M. Pogodin, historian and journalist
(1800–75), later acquired for Saltykov-Shchedrin
Public Library*

The manuscript contains no direct indications of the place and date of copying. However, some features of the language point to an origin in south-west Russia, while the script and the style of the illumination provide evidence for dating the manuscript, with a fair degree of certainty, to the late thirteenth century. It contains one miniature only. Christ, St Gregory and St Eustace fill a triple arch supported by pillars. In the spandrels over the arch are medallions with the Archangels Michael and Gabriel. Christ stands on a slight elevation, His right hand raised in blessing, His left holding a scroll. Iconographically, the figure is close to the Byzantine thirteenth-century type of standing Christ, of which there are examples in the Hermitage and the municipality of Galatina (Italy), and these again reproduce tenth- and eleventh-century Byzantine images, and stem ultimately from Early Christian sources. The tendency to revert to early models, strongly marked in Byzantine painting of the second half of the thirteenth century, was also apparent in Russian art of the time, notably in that of the Galich-Volynian Principality, which maintained particularly active contacts with the Byzantine world. An example is the icon of the Virgin of Sven, painted about 1288 either in Kiev or elsewhere in south-western Russia, which is clearly a copy of an eleventh-century image, probably Kievan or Byzantine in origin. It is close in composition and facial type to the present miniature.

The faces of Christ, St Gregory and St Eustace are remote and tranquil, the gaze turned inward, conveying a state of deep spiritual contemplation. This mood is enhanced by the soft shades of the painting of the faces, the ochres unbroken by any accents of light or colour. This style had its origins in the continuing influence of Byzantine art of the latter half of the eleventh and the twelfth centuries.

On the whole, however, the style of the present miniature has other characteristics that are far removed from the Byzantine tradition, but common to all Russian painting of the period of Mongol-Tartar rule. They are the use of strong colours and simple, precise lines. The three-dimensionality of Byzantine art is absent, and the flat, weightless outline is invested with great expressive power.

17 Chronicle of George Hamartolus

*Christ and Prince Michael of Tver
with His Mother Xenia*, f. 17v

Lenin Library, Moscow (transferred from the
collection of the Moscow Theological Academy,
Φ 173), ms 100
Tver, later 13th or first quarter of 14th century
Parchment 29×22.2 cm (11⅜×8⅝ in.); miniature
27.8×21 cm (10⅞×8¼ in.)
273 ff., 129 miniatures

PROVENANCE

*The Trinity Monastery of St Sergius; 1747 transferred
to the Trinity Theological Seminary; after 1814
Library of the Moscow Theological Academy; 1931
Lenin Library, Moscow*

Produced at Tver (now called Kalinin), this manuscript is an Old Slavonic version of a Byzantine world chronicle written by the monk Hamartolus in Constantinople about the middle of the ninth century. It covers the history of the world from the Creation to AD 842. A later author carried the story up to AD 948. The Old Slavonic translation of this text was well known in Bulgaria and Kiev, but no illuminated copies of its Greek, Bulgarian or Kievan versions have been preserved. The Tver manuscript reproduces an earlier Russian translation, probably made at Kiev, or a copy of it made at Vladimir.

The manuscript contains two full-page, facing miniatures and 127 small text-illustrations. The right-hand large miniature is a portrait of George Hamartolus; the left-hand page is illustrated. The leaf bears the signature of the illuminator, Prokopiy. The Prince and his mother appear as builders of a cathedral, hence they are painted in a church setting. This is probably a conventional representation of the Cathedral of Our Saviour of the Transfiguration at Tver, completed between 1285 and 1290. Enthroned at the centre is Christ to whom the cathedral was dedicated.

The impressive leaf evokes ninth- and tenth-century Byzantine art. The Greek original of the Chronicle, written at that period, may have contained a composition of Christ Enthroned shown with members of the Byzantine imperial house as donors: versions of this theme are known in contemporary mosaics, miniatures and ivory-carvings. The Tver illustration itself closely resembles the image in a late ninth-century mosaic in St Sophia in Constantinople, where Christ is represented with an emperor, perhaps Leo VI.

A lingering influence of the monumentality of Byzantine ninth- and tenth-century art can be detected in the composition, the faces, the fondness for rendering plastic form and for abundant folds in the drapery. To that extent the style is alien to the severely simple, even ascetic, mood of Russian art of its period, when Russian towns including Tver were under Mongol-Tartar domination. The imprint of the local Tver school is strong, however, in the rendering of the faces with thick, dark outlines, modelled with hatching in short white strokes, and with sharp, almost harsh, contrasts of light and shade.

18 The Theodore Lectionary

St Theodore Stratilates, f. 1v

Museum of History and Architecture, Yaroslavl,
ms 15718
Moscow, Rostov or Yaroslavl, 1320s
Parchment 36×25 cm (14⅛×9¾ in.)
223 ff., 5 miniatures (3 sewn in)

PROVENANCE

19th century, Cathedral of the Dormition, Yaroslavl;
1928 Museum of History and Architecture, Yaroslavl

The manuscript, commissioned by Bishop Prokhor, was in all probability copied between 1321 and 1327. Prokhor was Bishop of Rostov and also Archimandrite of the Monastery of Our Saviour of the Transfiguration at Yaroslavl. He is known to have supported Moscow at the time of its struggle for supremacy, and he led the procession at the dedication of the Dormition Cathedral in the Moscow Kremlin. Hence, any one of the three places – Rostov, Yaroslavl or Moscow – could have been the manuscript's place of origin.

The Lectionary is a sumptuous book, resplendently ornamented with five miniatures, six headpieces and a multitude of decorated initials. Gold was lavished on its illumination. Formerly the book had a precious wrought-metal cover, but this has been lost.

The initial page of the manuscript has an image of St Theodore Stratilates – a subject by no means common in a Gospel book, and executed on a special order: St Theodore Stratilates was the patron saint of Prince Theodore the Black of Yaroslavl (1240–99), and the manuscript was produced after the Prince's death as a tribute to his memory.

The figure of the warrior-saint is without background or frame, but is flanked by two graceful candelabra surmounted with peacocks. The Saint's right hand grasps his golden spear, his left a shield bearing an ounce, emblem of the princely house of Suzdal. In its rich colours and hieratic solemnity the miniature recalls representations in eleventh-century Kievan manuscripts, or in those of the Rostov-Suzdal Principality during the twelfth and early thirteenth centuries. The old tradition prevails in both the style and manner of execution. The thick, enamel-like colours are laid on evenly and provide no modelling. The figure seems to float weightlessly – an impression further strengthened by the outline of gold that seems to emit a faint radiance.

But alongside these traditional elements, the slender figure, small head and elegant feet, graceful posture and slightly S-shaped stance recall warrior-saints in the Parecclesion of the Chora Monastery in Constantinople, while the energy of the image, the sharply individualized treatment and the vigorous three-dimensional modelling of the face, with its strong contrasts of light and shade, directly link the painting with Byzantine art. This miniature is yet further evidence that the Russian artists of a number of different localities and schools were well acquainted with contemporary Byzantine painting.

19 The Theodore Lectionary

St John the Evangelist and St Prochoros,
f. 2v

Museum of History and Architecture, Yaroslavl,
ms 15718
Moscow, Rostov or Yaroslavl, 1320s
Parchment 34.8×25.2 cm (13⅝×9⅞ in.)
223 ff., 5 miniatures (3 sewn in)

The miniature shows St John dictating his gospel to St Prochoros in a church-interior, with an image of Christ on the vault of the central dome. The church is presumably one dedicated to Christ, and is probably intended to represent the Cathedral of the Monastery of the Transfiguration at Yaroslavl, where Bishop Prokhor, who commissioned the manuscript, was Archimandrite.

At top left, in a segment of starry sky, is a half-figure of Christ who is blessing and inspiring St John. The first words of the Gospel according to St John: 'In the beginning was the Word, and the Word was with God, and the Word was God', appear three times; they flow from Christ to the Evangelist, are transmitted by St John to his disciple, and finally are written by St Prochoros in the book.

Prochoros is given unusual prominence in this composition. Unlike the more customary image of him as a small figure bent over his writing, the Saint here appears as large and majestic as St John himself. This is readily accounted for by the fact that Prochoros is the patron of the bishop who commissioned the manuscript.

Like the preceding illustration (Pl. 18), this miniature is conspicuous for the beauty of its decoration, its rare and brilliant colours which include a malachite bluish-green and a cherry red, its profuse ornamentation, and an abundance of glittering gold, all of which resemble eleventh-century Kievan illuminations in such manuscripts as the Sviatoslav Codex (Pl. 6) or the Ostromir Lectionary (Pls. 1, 2). The manner is deliberately archaic, yet the imagery and overall style of the painting are inspired by the new ideas of early fourteenth-century Byzantine art.

The faces of Christ and St John, with their characteristic outlines sharply individualized, their sparkling eyes and animated, expressive features, recall the images, and even the facial types, of the frescoes of the Chora Monastery in Constantinople (*c.* 1320), while St Prochoros resembles the young saints in Byzantine wall-paintings and icons of the early fourteenth century. The same source explains St John's posture and the gesture of his hands, the form of the draperies, the intricate broad outlines, further complicated by the interplay of folds in the saints' cloaks, and lastly, the excellent modelling of the faces, hands and feet, achieved by fine gradations of colour – an evidence of the artist's keen interest in the three-dimensional.

These achievements of early fourteenth-century Byzantine art became known in Russia at this time, although only few artists made use of them.

20 The Siya Lectionary
The Mission of the Apostles, f. 172

Library of the USSR Academy of Sciences,
Leningrad (transferred from the collection of
Archaeographical Commission), ms 189
Moscow, 1340
Parchment 31.5×25 cm (12⅜×9¾ in.)
216 ff., 1 miniature

PROVENANCE

*1829 Library of the Monastery of St Antony on the
Siya, Archangel Province (discovered by P. Stroyev);
1903–27 Archangel; later transferred to Leningrad*

The Siya Lectionary, formerly adorned with two large miniatures, and with numerous animal-motif decorations, is provided with a detailed text giving the history of its production. It was completed in Moscow on 5 March 1340 and intended for the Monastery of the Dormition of the Virgin at Liavlia, on the River Dvin near Archangel. It is the work of two scribes, Melentiy and Prokosha. The name of the latter, which is a familiar form of Prokofiy, suggests that he was the younger of the two men, an apprentice or assistant. The illuminator John inscribed his name in the headpiece on folio 1 recto.

The scribe refers to the patron who commissioned the manuscript, the monk Ananiy, as 'one great among the servants of God'. This patron has been identified as Ivan I Kalita (1328–40), Grand-Prince of Moscow, known as the 'gatherer of the Russian lands', a man dedicated to the elevation of Moscow and the centralization of Russia. Shortly before his death, following the custom of the princely houses of Russia, Ivan I Kalita became a monk and received the monastic name of Ananiy.

The scribe compares the Grand-Prince of Moscow to the Byzantine emperors Constantine, Justinian and Manuel, and says that he made laws and gave justice, built many churches, taught the word of God to the people and even to priests, rooted out heresies and caused many books to be copied; also, that he loved the priesthood, and practised asceticism. The text grows into a eulogy of the mighty ruler leaving the world as a lowly monk.

Ivan I Kalita died twenty-six days after the completion of the manuscript, on 31 March 1340, and may either have read, or have heard read, this eloquent panegyric in his honour closing the magnificent volume created at his order.

That the manuscript was to be sent to a distant monastery in the north of Russia is in accordance with Ivan I Kalita's policy of strengthening and widening the influence of Moscow, and he was particularly interested in the rich lands of the North, which were under the dominion of Novgorod.

The subject of the miniature, Christ sending forth the Apostles to preach, is unusual for Russian illuminated books of Gospel readings, and may have been chosen to suggest the idea that Moscow was a most powerful state, and its Grand-Prince, a great ruler, was prepared to extend his good-will and protection to a distant northern monastery.

ШЕ ИСПОВѢДОША. ИПРѢ
ДАША ИПОМЕТЬ СКО
МУ ПИ ЛАТѸ ИГѢ
МОНОУ

21 The Siya Lectionary
The Adoration of the Magi

The Russian Museum, Leningrad, ms Др. гр. 8
Moscow, 1340
Parchment 30.6×22.2 cm (12×8⅝ in.)
Folio with the miniature cut out from the Siya
Lectionary (see Pl. 20)

The leaf with The Adoration of the Magi, once the initial page of the Siya Lectionary, was separated from the manuscript at some time, probably in the nineteenth century. Its connection with the Lectionary has only recently been demonstrated.

The subject of the Adoration is not a usual one for the opening page of a Russian book of Gospel readings, and its choice may be explained by the book's destination: the Monastery of the Dormition of the Virgin at Liavlia, as a personal gift from the Grand-Prince of Moscow.

Both miniatures in the codex, The Mission of the Apostles (Pl. 20) and The Adoration of the Magi, are full-page illustrations painted directly against the parchment without the customary gilt background, and are not framed in any way. The miniatures are the work of one artist; they are a rare specimen of early Moscow painting. In comparison with contemporary Byzantine works, the miniatures look archaic. The stocky figures, with short legs and massive heads, are clad in heavy fabrics with the drapery-folds barely indicated. The faces have large features, and all have the same fixed expression.

At the same time, the style of the two miniatures shows signs of a fresh approach. Both are painted in light, pure colours, applied in an almost transparent layer; a wide range of soft tones is used, forming a harmonious colour-scheme. The lines are gentle curves; harsh, sharply geometrical white high-lights are almost completely absent, and forms are modelled by more natural broad areas of colour. The handling shows greater ease and freedom than that of Russian thirteenth-century painting. The two Siya miniatures are like those in the Theodore Lectionary (Pls. 18, 19) in displaying, though not so mark-edly, a number of novel features derived from Byzantine painting of the first third of the fourteenth century. Both the manuscripts reflect the incipient revival of Russian painting after the period of Mongol-Tartar rule. They are evidence that Russian artistic life was about to resume its normal course, developing along the same lines as the art of the Byzantine world.

22 Lectionary
St John, f. 1v

Historical Museum, Moscow (acquired with the
Khludov collection), ms 30
Novgorod, mid-14th century
Parchment 31×23.5 cm (12⅛×9¼ in.)
213 ff., 4 miniatures

PROVENANCE

*The Khludov collection; 1917 Historical Museum,
Moscow (see also Pl. 12)*

The manuscript is a large codex with portraits of the Four Evangelists, and headpieces and initials with animal-decorations. It is datable to *c.* 1340–50, and was produced in Novgorod, probably in a scriptorium associated with Archbishop Vasiliy: this is suggested by a close stylistic affinity of the miniatures with the decorations of the 'Vasiliy Gate', a pair of large doors made for the Cathedral of St Sophia at Novgorod at the order of Archbishop Vasiliy in 1336. The scenes and figures on the doors (which are now in Alexandrov, near Moscow) were executed in gold on copper. There is another surviving example of the productions of the same workshop, slightly later in date (between 1340 and 1350), in the Holy Gate from the Likhachev collection (now in the Russian Museum, Leningrad), decorated in the same technique, with compositions of the Four Evangelists nearly identical to those in the Lectionary. These works of Novgorodian origin have an overall similarity of imagery and style owing much to the taste and personality of the patron, Archbishop Vasiliy, a man of lively and active disposition. An experienced statesman and administrator, he had also undertaken pilgrimages to Constantinople and the holy places of Palestine. He wrote on theology, and built a number of churches and furnished them with frescoes and icons. He is known to have invited a Greek painter to Novgorod for this purpose.

The miniatures of the Lectionary, like many other such Novgorodian productions, clearly show contemporary Byzantine influence. A number of features – the three-dimensional treatment of architectural elements, the figures of Byzantine type in full robes with a multitude of folds, the abundance of minute highlights creating an effect similar to the play of light and shade, the modelling of forms, and the variety of foreshortenings – all produce a style close to that of Byzantine miniatures such as the Gospels in the Vienna Library (Theol. Gr. 300), or the Gospels of 1335 from the St John Monastery on Patmos, or the Gospels of the Great Lavra on Mount Athos (A. 76). But Byzantine styles appear in Novgorodian works in a form rather quaintly adapted to local taste: they acquire a monumental quality alien to book-illumination, alongside a certain harshness and even exaggeration. Though oriented towards Byzantine models, Novgorodian art tended to preserve local tradition in all its fresh force and liveliness.

23 The Orsha Lectionary
St Luke, f. 42

Central Library of the Ukrainian SSR Academy of
Sciences, ms TA. II. 555
Novgorod (?), 14th century
Parchment 26.4×19.4 cm (10⅜×7⅝ in.); miniature
21×14.5 cm (8¼×5⅝ in.)
142 ff., 2 miniatures

The Orsha Lectionary comes from a monastery near the town of Orsha in the west, an area that was once in the Polotsk-Smolensk Principality. To the north the Polotsk-Smolensk Principality bordered that of Novgorod, and the art of the two states had much in common. Their mural-painting, in particular, is similar: the twelfth- and early thirteenth-century frescoes of Polotsk and Smolensk churches closely resemble Novgorod murals. There are reasons to suppose that the two schools of painting maintained close contacts until the fourteenth century.

We have hardly any specimens of fourteenth-century painting from western Russia. The miniatures of the Orsha Lectionary are therefore unusual – perhaps even unique – examples of the work done in that region. They bear a strong resemblance to mid-fourteenth-century illumination in the Novgorodian Lectionary from the Khludov collection (Pl. 22, fig. xi), and in another Novgorodian book from the same period (fig. xii). These resemblances are to be observed in the iconography and composition, which are practically identical in all the three cases; in the architectural elements (of which the most elaborate are in Pl. 22); in the forms of the furniture – the chairs, tables and lecterns; in the manner of painting – rich and broad, somewhat coarse, and bounded by the stiff outline; and lastly, in the sumptuous, full robes with a profusion of folds and light areas, that are common in Byzantine miniatures from the earlier years of the fourteenth century, and especially characteristic of those from the mid-fourteenth century.

The miniatures of the Orsha Lectionary, while they have close affinities with the Novgorodian miniatures mentioned above – being created in a similar artistic climate, where Byzantine models were imitated – are at the same time adapted to local tradition. Compared with Novgorodian examples, the miniatures of the Orsha Lectionary are softer, and lack the expressive force, assertiveness and harshness of the Novgorod style.

24 The Anthology of Sylvester

Two Scenes from the Life of St Boris,
f. 128v

Central State Archives of Ancient Documents,
Moscow (transferred from the collection of the
Synodal Printing House), ms 53
Novgorod, latter half of 14th century
Parchment 30×22.5 cm (11¾×8¾ in.)
216 ff., 22 miniatures

This Novgorod manuscript is decorated with seventeen miniatures depicting episodes from the Lives of Saints Boris and Gleb, and five miniatures illustrating the apocryphal Life of Abraham (from the Palaea version of the Old Testament). The captions provide a detailed commentary on the action of the scenes and are disposed like friezes.

The present manuscript is the only illuminated copy of the Lives of the two Russian saints. Its miniatures are reminiscent of the small scenes placed in the border of Russian icons representing episodes of the life of the saint portrayed. Like those scenes, they are painted in a lively narrative style, and in a free, summary manner, with details rapidly sketched in, and bright, decorative colours. This manner remained practically unaltered throughout the fourteenth century. Only a few details of the present miniature, such as the elongated oval shape of the faces, the receding chins, a general lack of symmetry in the features, and the sketchy outlines, point to the second half of the century as the date of their production.

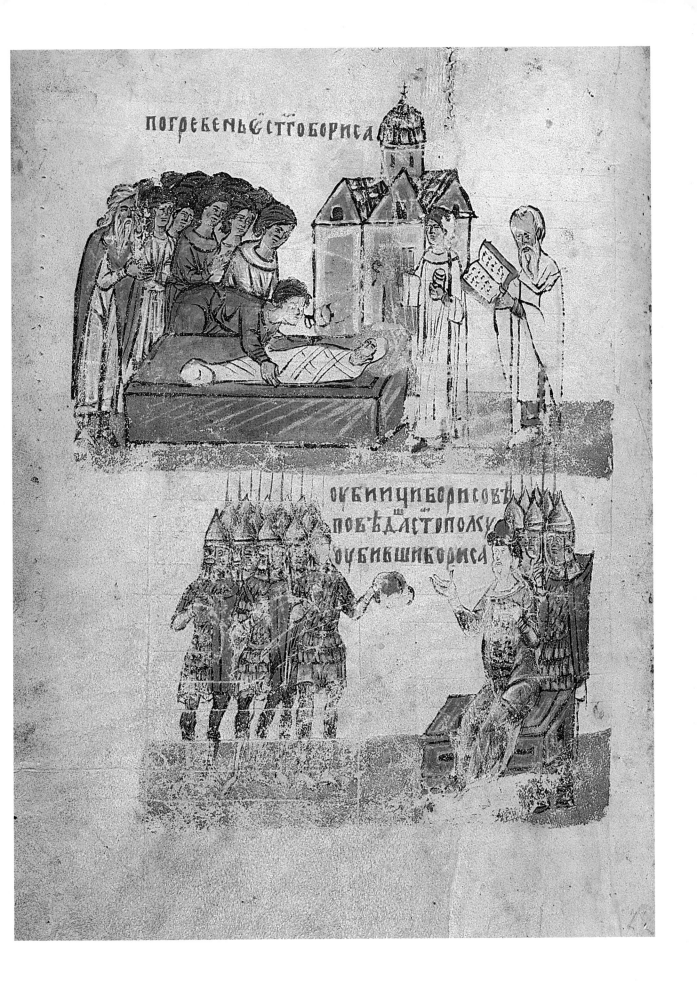

25 The Anthology of Sylvester

Two Scenes from the Life of St Gleb, f. 132

Central State Archives of Ancient Documents,
Moscow (transferred from the collection of the
Synodal Printing House), ms 53
Novgorod, latter half of 14th century
Parchment 30×22.5 cm (11¾×8¾ in.)
216 ff., 22 miniatures

Descriptions of the scenes in the Lives of Saints Boris and Gleb are given by the captions. Above, Gleb's horse has stumbled and broken its leg. Below, Gleb and his companions are on the river-bank, about to board a boat.

The miniatures are lively and graphic, characteristic of the style of Russian local art. The appeal of this type of miniature lies in the purity and brightness of the colours, the clarity of the outlines, the balance of the composition of the groups, and an almost fairy-tale narrative atmosphere. Art of this kind may be considered too simple and undemanding, judged by the sophisticated standards of Byzantium; it is rooted in the folklore tradition of Russian culture.

СТЫИ ГЛѢБ Ѣ ДОТЪ НА КОНѢ ИПО ТЦЕ САКОНЬ ИМАЛО
ИМ СМУНОГУ И ПОИ ДЕ ВНОСАДЪ

СТЫИ ГЛѢБ Ѣ ВЪ ЛѢZ ЕТЪ ВЪ НАСА

26 Psalter, known as The Psalter of Ivan the Terrible

The Temple Musician Asaph, f. 169

Lenin Library, Moscow (transferred from the
collection of the Trinity Cathedral of St Sergius,
Φ 304), ms M. 8662
Novgorod, last third of 14th century
Parchment 31.5×24.5 cm (12⅜×9⅝ in.)
324 ff., 2 miniatures

PROVENANCE

*16th century, Vestry of the Trinity Monastery of
St Sergius; 1931 Lenin Library, Moscow*

The large and richly ornamented manuscript with two miniatures, one representing King David and the other Asaph, was made in Novgorod to judge by certain features of the language of the text, the type of ornamentation and the style of the miniature. Yet we learn from the inscription that the Tsar and Grand-Prince Ivan IV the Terrible presented the Psalter to St Sergius' Trinity Monastery at Zagorsk. It is probable that the book was brought from Novgorod to Moscow at the command of Ivan IV the Terrible in 1570, and was placed in St Sergius' Trinity Monastery later.

Asaph is depicted half-length, with broad, rapid strokes, in the manner of fresco-painting, under an ogee arch as if in a five-domed church building composed of animal-motif interlace, serpentine ribbons and writhing monsters twisted into elaborate knots. The convention of depicting church buildings as constructed of decorative interlace motifs had been favoured as early as the eleventh century by Kievan artists (as in the Sviatoslav Codex, Pl. 6); but Kievan illuminators used a different type of interlace, originating in the Byzantine tradition and formed of flowers, leaves and geometrical figures. In the Novgorodian miniature, the interlace is distinctly northern in character, with animal- and monster-shapes closer to the ornamental fantasies of medieval Europe, especially Scandinavia, than to Byzantine examples.

Animal-decoration gained a wide diffusion all over the Russian lands in the thirteenth century, reaching its peak in the fourteenth. Its most expressive form was elaborated, however, in the northern regions, notably in Novgorod. The miniatures of the Psalter of Ivan IV the Terrible are among the best examples of Novgorodian interlace: ingenious and intricate in design, perfect in composition and calligraphically precise in execution. In his rendering of the fantastic animals, with their lithe movements and merciless grip, the illuminator gave a certain mannered elegance to the twisted forms. The tension is present in every knot, and nowhere is it resolved. But the overall interlinking lends harmony and balance to the chaos of forms. The horrifying and the attractive appear here side by side like good and evil in life. The light tones of the colouring and the clarity of the composition serve to neutralize the theme of animal ferocity in the decorative motifs, and to create a bright and joyous effect.

27 Lectionary

The Four Evangelists, f. 1v

Historical Museum, Moscow (transferred from the
collection of the Chudov Monastery), ms 2
Moscow, late 14th century
Parchment 29.5×21.5 cm (11½×8⅜ in.); miniature
24×17 cm (9⅜×6⅝ in.)
149 ff., 1 miniature

PROVENANCE

*19th century, the Chudov Monastery, Moscow; 1899
Synodal (Patriarchal) Library; 1920 transferred to
Historical Museum, Moscow*

The manuscript from the library of the Chudov Monastery (Monastery of the
Miracle of St Michael) in Moscow was not written in the scriptorium of that
monastery, but entered its library in the sixteenth century as the gift of 'Priest
Joseph'. Moscow, however, is undoubtedly the manuscript's place of production.

The opening page of the codex is painted with the portraits of the Four
Evangelists, each of the compositions unframed and closely adjoining. The
whole leaf has a double border of red and light brown, like an icon. The
illuminator probably took as a model a small composite icon consisting of
several subjects, each in a separate compartment; such icons were common in
late fourteenth-century Moscow (for example the Four-Part Icon, or the Six-
Part Icon, both ascribed to the workshop of Theophanes the Greek). This
source is suggested not only by the composition of the miniature, but also by
its general mood, the character of the imagery, and certain features of the style.

An atmosphere of high emotion and inspiration pervades the scenes, conveyed by the expression of the Evangelists' faces and their attitudes, by the
carelessly disarranged folds of their robes and even by the backgrounds with
buildings or mountains that crowd around the figures. The brushwork is rapid
and flowing, the colours are clear and transparent, saturated with light.
Numerous strokes and touches of white are used to convey light, which is
intended to invest matter with spirit. The lines are dynamic, smooth, mobile;
the forms, small and fragile; matter, permeated with light, loses its heavy
materiality.

The miniature is imbued with an intense and exalted spirituality, typical of
Late Byzantine art, and copied by Russian painters from Theophanes the
Greek and other Greek artists working in Russia, as well as from the icons and
illuminated manuscripts brought to Moscow from Constantinople.

28 The Kiev Psalter (Spiridon Psalter)

Illustrations to Psalm 21:17: *Christ Surrounded by Dog-headed Soldiers* and *The Crucifixion*; and to Psalm 21:19: *Soldiers Divide Christ's Garments among Them*, f. 28

Saltykov-Shchedrin Public Library, Leningrad
(transferred from the collection of the Society of
Lovers of Ancient Literature), ms F. 6
Written in Kiev by a scribe from Moscow;
miniatures probably produced in Moscow, 1397
Parchment 30×24.5 cm (11¾×9⅝ in.)
229 ff., 314 miniatures

PROVENANCE

*Early 16th century to early 1870s, private or church
collections in Wilno (Vilnius), Grodno and Warsaw;
1874–81 collection of Prince P. Viazemsky; later,
collection of Count S. Sheremetyev, who donated it
to the Society of Lovers of Ancient Literature; 1932
Saltykov-Shchedrin Public Library, Leningrad*

The Kiev Psalter, one of the most luxurious and magnificently decorated of Russian manuscript books, contains more than three hundred miniatures scattered through the margins as well as numerous other ornaments. The codex is large in size, as was customary for a Russian liturgical book, and differs markedly from illuminated Byzantine psalters in its grand scale, its solemn style and its great splendour.

An inscription by the scribe, Archdeacon Spiridon, states that the manuscript was produced in 1397 'at the command of Bishop Mikhail' in Kiev: hence the name Kiev Psalter by which it is commonly known. Research has shown that the scribe and his patron had both recently arrived in Kiev from Moscow; Mikhail, who had been elected Bishop of Smolensk in 1383, was formerly a monk in the Simonov Monastery in Moscow and kept up his ties with that city. Both men arrived in Kiev among the retinue of the Metropolitan Cyprian during his visit there in 1396–7. It was then that the Psalter was written. Its illuminations, however, are not by Spiridon and were probably executed in Moscow after Cyprian's return there. Hence the name by which the manuscript is traditionally designated is belied by the style of its decoration, carried out in a Moscow scriptorium by an artist of the Moscow school.

The miniatures take the form of small scenes or individual figures providing marginal commentary on the Psalms. A thin red line connects the miniature with the text to which it relates. The illustrations on folio 28 refer to Psalm 22:16, 18 (Septuagint 21:17, 19). The group of Christ amid dog-headed soldiers in the right margin relates to the words: 'For dogs have encompassed me, the assembly of the wicked have inclosed me'. The scene at lower right relates to the line: 'They pierced my hands and my feet'. In the lower margin is a group of soldiers dividing Christ's garments: 'They part my garments among them and cast lots upon my vesture'.

на

Ѡвѣщошащаоустаⷭвоѩ . ꙗколⷷ
въвъсхыщлющинⷬкрлꙗ
Иководлⷢниꙗсꙗирасыплша
сꙗвсꙗкⷭстиⷨоꙗ . быⷭцѣмое
ꙗкⷪвоскⷮлапосредеутревⷶю
его . ишениꙗкⷪскⷪцделькрⷶⷮпо
стьмоꙗ . иꙗзыкъмоипⷪналпе
гортаниюеⷨоⷱ . ивъперⷭтьсь
ⷨⷬтисведлⷷⷨесн . ꙗкⷪбни
дошлⷶщапⷭсниⷨнозн . снеⷨьлⷪ
клⷷⷭⷮвыѡдержашаⷨ . исⷬкоⷫ
шлⷪⷱⷮⷨⷩⷩⷪⷮⷨⷩ

Исуѣтошавсꙗкⷭстиⷨоꙗ
Тнⷤесⷪⷮⷬншлⷩⷬⷷⷢрⷫⷣшⷩⷩⷬ
Разьдѣлншлⷬнⷬⷢⷩⷨⷩⷪⷬⷭⷮⷨⷷⷪⷬⷷ

29 The Kiev Psalter (Spiridon Psalter)

Fable of the Sweetness of This World;
or, *Fable of the Unicorn*, f. 197

Saltykov-Shchedrin Public Library, Leningrad
(transferred from the collection of the Society of
Lovers of Ancient Literature), ms F. 6
Written in Kiev by a scribe from Moscow;
miniatures probably produced in Moscow, 1397
Parchment 30×24.5 cm (11¾×9⅝ in.)
229 ff., 314 miniatures

The illustration is based on the Fable of the Sweetness of This World, also known as the Fable of the Unicorn, from 'Barlaam and Joasaph', a Christian religious romance popular in the Middle Ages, the Greek version of which is ascribed to St John of Damascus (675–749). No connecting line indicates the exact words of the Psalm to which the miniature relates; the artist probably had in mind the lines, 'O Lord, what is man?… Man is like a breath, his days are like a passing shadow…' (Psalm 143:3, 4).

The legends written in small script in vermilion explain the meaning of each detail. A man is trying to escape from a unicorn, which is a symbol of Death. He climbs a tree and, thinking himself safe, tastes with delight the honey dripping from its branches. The tree, as we learn from the captions, is symbolic of the life of man, and its dense branches, of the 'alluring temptations' of this world. The man is, however, unaware that two mice, one white and one black (Day and Night), are incessantly gnawing at the base of the trunk, and that the earth opens wide near it, revealing a bottomless pit wherein dwells a beast with gaping maw (Hell).

All the miniatures in the manuscript are painted with skill. The figures are light and dynamic, free and natural; the graceful compositions fit the margin-space beautifully; the colours give a bright and festive look to each page. The garments are shot through with golden rays symbolizing divine light.

Many features of the style, such as the composition, the type of colouring and the use of gold hatching, are not merely close to the manner of eleventh-century Byzantine artists, but are identical. The illuminator of the Psalter must have used as a model an earlier Byzantine Psalter, probably a source similar to that used for a fourteenth-century Psalter now in Baltimore in the Walters Art Gallery (cod. W 733). Nevertheless, the miniatures of the 1397 Kiev Psalter could not be mistaken for eleventh-century work, but have a distinctive quality of their period in the lively expressions and gestures, and even the facial features. The imagery and style are charged with dynamism and a heightened spirituality. The brushwork is rapid and spontaneous. These features are common in late fourteenth-century art of the Byzantine world, whether in Constantinople or in the Balkans – for example in the frescoes at the Church of Ivanovo near Ruse in Bulgaria, or at the Church of the Assumption at Volotovo near Novgorod, or the miniatures of the Psalter of Ivan IV the Terrible (Pl. 26).

+ прилежа фи оубо ли тигосемоу. итаковомоу
работаюфи лютомоу влꙗце. благо и нꙋколого
бивꙗ оумоувредно, дальшисꙗ нисего жиꙗ при
ложнисꙗ вефе

инꙑе горписанїи, ксꙗписовешаше дале боутье моувсеꙗ. вꙑеже течашес нсꙗ
в великоу оубꙗоꙋто впаде пропасть. внегда мевпа стисꙗемоу внꙗо издарвонꙗское по
хитносꙗксꙗписоꙗꙋрꙗдаше ина дꙗ ссобꙗсоеꙗ по сбоуꙗвердꙗ. мнꙗше процеевꙗ ми
рꙑвꙑтиивтвердꙗими. ини трꙗе сꙗидꙗвꙗмꙗ шꙗни стлоусоꙋедꙗноу, роꙋроꙋгоꙋ чермоꙋ
погри глꙗюꙗфинепрестꙗнꙗдꙗрꙗва, е гоꙗ тꙗбоꙋхиꙗласа. не лꙗико вꙗмꙗлꙗприꙗни
юꙗшемꙗсꙗима снꙗе псꙗсо ренꙗти. посмо трꙗвꙗне ꙗвꙗдно пропастꙗи. вꙗдꙗ медꙗтꙗ
шꙗма видꙗние ноꙗ медꙗ вꙗшюꙗша народꙗꙗꙗ
рꙗтоꙗча ноꙋꙗтꙗстрашно дꙗꙗтꙗмоꙋ по трет
грꙗдꙗше. сꙗгꙗребꙗепꙗꙗсꙗинꙗ стꙗепенꙗꙗ
нꙗнемꙗжебꙗꙗше ноꙗ сꙗвоноꙋꙗтвердꙗи. сꙗ
л главꙑꙗшипꙗвꙑшестꙗнꙑꙗписꙗшꙗдꙗнаме
стоꙗꙗ. иꙋꙗзꙗꙗочима биꙗдравꙗотꙗвꙗинꙗа
вꙗдꙗомꙗ маломедꙗ исꙗплоꙗчꙗ. остꙗвꙗленꙗ
пꙗꙗфꙗиꙗоꙋбоꙗдꙗержꙗꙗ фꙗ ингеꙗгоꙗвꙗꙗадꙗ. иꙗтꙗ
дꙗ исꙗитоꙗсꙗлебꙗоꙋꙗстꙗремꙗивꙗсꙗладꙗ
мала ме доꙋ оꙗного ...

БИШИВСѦВЛГЫШИОѦ . ИПОГОЦ
БИШИВСАСТОЦМѦИШЛѦДШИ
ШОЕН . ИКОѦЗЪРѦБЪТВОНЕШИ
СЛА . КЛ . К . ПѦ . ДВ . РИГ . КГОЛѦ

ЛГВНЪГЬБЪШЮННЛОЦУЛѦ
ЮЦЕШИННЛ ОПОЛУЕНІЕ
ИПЕРСТЫШЮНЛЛБРѦНЬ ,
ИЛѦТЫШЮНПРИБѢЖИЩЕ
ШОЕ , ЗЛСТОЦПНИКЪШИН , ИН
ЗБЛВИТЕЛЬШИН . ЗЛЩИТИТЕ
ШИН , ИНЛНЬЮЦПОВЛ . ПОВИННЙ
ИНЛНЮШЮПОШѦ . ГНУТІЕСТ
УЛВКЪЫѦКОСКАЗЛЛСѦ ЕСНЕШ
ЛИСНУЛВУЫѦКОВШЕНѢНѦЕШНЙ

сꙗꙗꙗдрꙗво
е мꙗтие
ꙗлꙗꙋꙗе

сꙗепоꙗвꙗецꙗ
лꙗ стꙗимꙗꙗ
пꙗвꙗлꙗꙗатꙗоꙗчꙗи

инꙗроꙗдоꙋбоꙗшꙗбрꙗдꙗе
смꙗрꙗтꙗ

дꙗ
нꙗоꙋꙗ

пропасть ме е мирꙗсꙗ. исꙗплꙗне всꙗекꙗи
го несмертоносꙗдꙗ сꙗтꙗни.

отꙗ мира дꙗоꙋмꙗꙗ ванꙗе трꙗашꙗноꙋꙗто да оꙋꙗбꙋꙗбꙗсꙗ
дꙗ дꙗюꙗꙗдꙗ. ꙗꙗ дꙗ боꙗ стоꙋꙗ хиꙗмꙗсꙗтавꙗленꙗие
ꙋꙗлꙗꙋꙗ.

30 The Pereyaslavl Gospels
Christ in Majesty, f. 6

Saltykov-Shchedrin Public Library, Leningrad,
ms Fn I. 21
Pereyaslavl-Zalessky, late 14th or early 15th century
(probably first quarter of 15th century)
Parchment 24×17.5 cm (9⅜×6⅞ in.); miniature
21×14 cm (8¼×5½ in.)
166 ff., 5 miniatures

PROVENANCE

*16th century, St Nicholas Monastery, Pereyaslavl-
Zalessky; early 19th century, collection of Count
F. Tolstoy; 1830 acquired by Public Library,
St Petersburg*

The city of Pereyaslavl-Zalessky, where the manuscript was produced, was one of the ancient cities of north-western Russia. It was incorporated into the principality of Moscow in 1302, but its loss of independence did not cause it to sink into insignificance; it retained a considerable political and cultural importance. Ecclesiastic councils and royal assemblies were held in the city; and the great Byzantine painter Theophanes the Greek is known to have worked there.

The artists of Pereyaslavl followed in the wake of the Moscow school. But for all its advanced tendencies, art there is apt to display the imprint of provincial taste.

It was in this artistic milieu that the best of all surviving Pereyaslavl manuscripts was created, a book of Gospels commissioned by Savva, Abbot of the Monastery of the Presentation of the Virgin, and copied by a scribe who calls himself Deacon Zenobius.

The five miniatures are an image of Christ in Majesty and portraits of the Four Evangelists. The portraits are obviously the work of an illuminator of the local school while the image of Christ shows the hand of another, much superior artist. The sophisticated iconography and high level of professional skill make the miniature one of the most interesting works of the Moscow school of the late fourteenth and early fifteenth centuries. The iconographic type of Christ enthroned in a mandorla was common at the time, both in icons (notably those intended for church screens) and in miniatures by Moscow artists.

There is a similarity with Byzantine art in the restrained and concentrated image, the narrow, oval face with fine, strongly marked features, lit as by a heavenly light and modelled by pictorial means, the profusion of drapery-folds creating an intricate pattern. These features have no analogies in Russian painting. The artist of the miniature, who worked in a subtle and somewhat dry manner, must have faithfully imitated a Byzantine model of a kind quite different from the art of Theophanes the Greek.

The miniature owes its appeal not to any special expressive force, but to the sense of calm, serene detachment, of perfect spiritual harmony achieved through contemplation, which emanates from the image of Christ.

31 Lectionary
St Mark, f. 44v

Historical Museum, Moscow, ms 3651
Novgorod, last third of 14th century
Parchment 29×22.5 cm (11⅜×8¾ in.); miniature
20.5×16 cm (8×6¼ in.)
163 ff., 3 miniatures

PROVENANCE

19th century, library of the Obolensky family; 1845
presented to the archives of the Ministry of Foreign
Affairs by M. Obolensky; latter half of 19th century,
Armoury, Moscow; 1922 Historical Museum,
Moscow

This book of readings from the Gospels for church use is of fairly large size, as was usual for Russian liturgical books. Its illumination consists of four head-pieces and numerous decorated initials, in addition to three miniatures. Originally there was a fourth miniature, but this has not survived.

There is no record of the names of the scribe or his patron, or reference to the church or monastery for which the manuscript was copied, and no indication of the date of its production. Information may, however, be gleaned from such evidence as the character of the script and the ornamentation, and features of the language. Linguistic research, as well as the study of the types and style of animal-decorations, point to Novgorod as the manuscript's place of production. Palaeography shows that it was copied in the latter half of the fourteenth century; and analysis of the miniatures further narrows the period to the last third of the century.

St Mark is represented standing, with a scroll in one hand. This is the iconography of the Prophets, and unusual in the case of an Evangelist.

The figure has a monumental quality, resembling a detail of a mural-painting. The style, as well as the treatment of the image – the choice of facial type, and a complex psychological approach to character-portrayal – are alien to Novgorodian painting, but close to the art of Serbia and Macedonia. It may be conjectured that the miniature was painted by an artist from the Balkans, one of a group working in Novgorod in the latter half of the fourteenth century. Frescoes by this group have been preserved in some of the Novgorodian churches, for instance the Church of Our Saviour at Kovalevo and the Church of the Nativity-in-the-Field. Possibly this manuscript book was intended for use in the same church that the artist was decorating with frescoes.

32 Lectionary

St Luke, f. 89v

Historical Museum, Moscow (transferred from the
collection of the Synodal Printing House), ms 71
Pskov, 1409
Parchment 32×24.5 cm (12½×9⅝ in.); miniature
26×17 cm (10⅛×6⅝ in.)
219 ff., 3 miniatures

PROVENANCE

17th century, Library of the Synodal Printing House;
18th century, transferred to the Synodal (Patriarchal)
Library; 1920 acquired for Historical Museum,
Moscow

The manuscript opens with a long 'foreword' by the scribe containing the date
of the codex, 1409, and the name of the patron, the monk Theodore. Theodore
is said to have commissioned the manuscript for the Monastery of St Nicholas
in Zavelichye – that is, in Pskov – and he probably belonged to that monastery.
The copying is described as being done in the reign of Vasiliy Dmitriyevich,
Grand-Prince of All Russia, and during the metropolitanate of Cyprian.
Several persons of high rank who were in office at Pskov and Novgorod at the
time are listed: Bishop Ivan of Novgorod; Roman Sidorovich, Mayor of Pskov,
whose name appears in the chronicles of 1407 to 1415; two Pskovian leaders,
Ivan Garb and Marcha; and Semion, Abbot of the St Nicholas Monastery at
Pskov. The scribe finally identifies himself as 'Luke the great sinner, Deacon of
the Church of the Holy Trinity', and ends with an appeal to the reader to
correct any errors and not to blame him for them, for 'the Lord will enlighten
you and instruct you'. The clearly legible handwriting reveals Luke as a scribe
of skill and experience.

The illumination consists of a great number of headpieces and initials
decorated with animal-motifs of a type close to the Novgorodian, all executed
with imagination and technical mastery, and three author-portraits only, of
Matthew, Luke and Mark. The Evangelists are shown writing the Gospels in
the interiors of triple-domed churches, their outlines filled with fantastic
monsters in a dense interlace like those of Novgorodian manuscripts such as
the Psalter of Ivan IV the Terrible (Pl. 26).

The green backgrounds are probably of later date (possibly sixteenth century) as are the inscriptions in black lettering, and the lines around the Saints'
haloes. Characteristic of the style of Pskov are the Saints' expression of
restraint, the facial types – a narrow oval, with strongly marked features and
close-set eyes – the overall proportions of the lean, narrow-shouldered figures,
a certain stiffness of outline and angularity of the drapery-folds, the minute
hatching used for the highlights, and a general lack of freedom together with an
obvious archaizing tendency. Although the miniatures of the 1409 Lectionary
show some influence from the contemporary Byzantine world in the mildness
of the faces and fragility of the figures, still the artist was guided predominantly
by a deeply rooted veneration for ancient local traditions.

33 The Four Gospels

St Mark, f. 58v

Lenin Library, Moscow (acquired with the
Rumiantsev collection), ms 118
Moscow, 1401
Parchment 17×12.5 cm (6⅝×4⅞ in.); miniature
12×8.5 cm (4⅝×3¼ in.)
215 ff., 4 miniatures and a drawing (? 17th century)

PROVENANCE

*1825 bought from K. Averin, a merchant, by
K. Kalaidovich for Count N. Rumiantsev*

This small manuscript is written in a neat script. Each of the Gospels opens
with a portrait of its author. The elegant miniatures, so exquisitely executed
and distinguished by a type of composition unusual in Russian art of this
period, suggest the hand of an accomplished artist employed by an important
patron.

According to the scribe's note, work on the book was completed on 10 June
1401. Although the writer does not name the place where he lived and worked,
there is every reason to suppose that it was Moscow. Evidence for this is to be
found in his superb and delicately executed miniatures, showing both a strong
Byzantine influence and iconographic details peculiar to the Moscow school
(for example, the landscape in the miniature with St John, and the architectural
motifs in the three other scenes).

The name of the illuminator is unknown: he may have been Byzantine, or a
Russian painter trained in Byzantine art. It is extremely difficult to distinguish
between the works of Moscow and Byzantine masters of the time, since both
schools display the traits of the Orthodox world in general.

The miniatures of the 1401 Gospels have a close affinity with a special trend
of contemporary Byzantine art (such as we find in the wall-paintings of the
churches of Mistra in south Greece) which sought to revive early fourteenth-
century concepts as they were expressed in the paintings at the Chora Monastery in Constantinople. Among the characteristic features of this art we find
small, fine forms, elaborate architectural backgrounds with solitary cypresses
and palms, well-proportioned figures with small, exquisitely executed heads
and robes that are intricately modelled with delicately accentuated folds.

34 The Four Gospels
St Luke, f. 112

Lenin Library, Moscow (transferred from the
collection of the Trinity Monastery of St Sergius,
Ф 304), ms M. 8665
Moscow, early 15th century
Parchment 27.5×21 cm (10¾×8¼ in.); miniature
19×13 cm (7⅜×5 in.)
242 ff., 4 miniatures

PROVENANCE

Vestry of the Trinity Monastery of St Sergius; 1931
Lenin Library, Moscow

A large manuscript, this is written on fine parchment and, even among the
superb illuminations produced in Moscow in the late fourteenth and early
fifteenth centuries, its four miniatures of the Evangelists stand out as especially
refined. The manuscript was undoubtedly executed on a special order by the
most skilled scribes and illuminators. It is a pity that it contains no notes which
might throw light on the history of its production, but certain details indicate
that it was produced in one of the best Moscow scriptoria in the early fifteenth
century, and that it was subsequently given to the Trinity Monastery of St
Sergius.

The illuminator was a contemporary of the great Russian painter Andrei
Rublev, and the work of the two artists has certain features in common,
reflecting the artistic atmosphere of that time. These are similarities in the
delicate treatment of the faces, in the smooth, flowing lines, in the subtle and
radiant colours, and in the gentle warmth. These characteristics are typical of
the art of Moscow, and also of Serbia and Byzantium, in the early fifteenth
century.

The conception and rendering, however, differ considerably from the style
of Rublev. There is an impulsive agitation about the nervous, wavering lines
and contours; the colours are exaggeratedly refined. The Saints gaze anxiously,
with piercing eyes. Compared with Rublev's art, this master's works seem a
more intimate echo of the grand style of the time.

35 Lectionary

St Luke, f. 126v

Gorky Library, Moscow University, Moscow,
ms 2 Вд 42
Moscow, late 14th or early 15th century
Parchment 24×18 cm (9⅜×7 in.); miniature
17.5×13.4 cm (6⅞×5¼ in.)
260 ff., 4 miniatures (2 probably 19th century)

PROVENANCE

*1840 bought in Yaroslavl for P. Aktov; later,
collection of Count S. Stroganov; 1840s acquired by
the Library of Moscow University*

The manuscript contains no indication as to where and when it was created. Its miniatures allow us, however, to attribute it to the Moscow school of the turn of the fourteenth century.

Two of the miniatures depict St Mark and St Luke, each shown with St Sophia, Divine Wisdom, who taught and inspired the Evangelists. Her robe billows behind her and she seems as if descending from heaven. The image of St Sophia is seldom encountered in Russian art of this or the preceding periods (one of the rare examples is provided by the frescoes in the Novgorod Church of the Dormition at Volotovo), but it was a constant feature of Serbian murals and manuscripts of the fourteenth and the first third of the fifteenth century. A Serbian miniature may have served as a model for the Moscow artist.

The style of the miniature is also quite unusual. It should be borne in mind that at the turn of the fourteenth century there were many foreign artists working in Russia, representing such a diversity of styles that all new influences were assimilated with remarkable speed.

The miniatures in this manuscript are notable for their elaborate architectural backgrounds. Though to some extent conventionalized and illogically arranged, the architectural details are presented three-dimensionally and produce a spatial effect. This is typical of Byzantine art of the period.

The unusual iconography, the classical porticos and columns, St Sophia's billowing robe resembling the drapery found in the Chora Monastery mosaics, and the bright, pure colours are all reminiscent of the compositions in early fourteenth-century Byzantine painting which were revived in the late fourteenth and early fifteenth centuries.

36 The Khitrovo Lectionary
St Matthew, f. 44v

Lenin Library, Moscow (transferred from the
collection of the Trinity Monastery of St Sergius,
Φ 304), ms M. 8657
Moscow, late 14th or early 15th century
Parchment 32.2×24.8 cm (12⅝×9¾ in.); miniature
22×17 cm (8⅝×6⅝ in.)
300 ff., 8 miniatures

The Khitrovo Lectionary is one of the most famous of early Russian
manuscripts. The identity of the scribe, the illuminator and the patron who
commissioned the work are all unknown, and its history can be traced only
from the comparatively late date of 1677, when the Tsar Fiodor Alexeyevich
(1661–82) gave the book to the Boyar Bogdan Khitrovo (hence the name by
which it is traditionally known), and the latter, in his turn, presented it to the
Trinity Monastery of St Sergius, where it was kept until 1931.

On the evidence of a note by Khitrovo attached to the manuscript, the
Lectionary had once belonged to the Tsar's family. It was probably ordered by
a Russian prince.

The general appearance of the Lectionary, its language, script, miniatures
and ornamentation, allow it to be attributed to the Moscow school, and to be
dated to the first years of the fifteenth century.

The manuscript contains eight miniatures, four of which portray the Evangelists and four their emblems – an eagle (St John), a man with wings (St
Matthew), a winged lion (St Mark), and a winged ox (St Luke). The signs of the
Evangelists represented on separate folios are not known in Russian manuscripts before the Khitrovo Lectionary. All are depicted in round medallions
against a gold background.

The folios are lavishly decorated; the initials are composed of various
animals and bird-shapes, friendly looking and at play. There is none of the
tension so typical of animal ornament. The animals and birds in these miniatures are good-natured and beautiful creatures, straight from a fairy-tale.

The folios with miniatures seem to radiate light, and the atmosphere is one of
utter calm and peace. The Saints appear as harmony and grace incarnate. Such
treatment is characteristic of icons and frescoes by Andrei Rublev, and it is
therefore quite possible that he was the artist of the Khitrovo Lectionary.

ō ματθε
ιος

44

37 The Khitrovo Lectionary
The Sign of St Matthew, f. 43v

Lenin Library, Moscow (transferred from the
collection of the Trinity Monastery of St Sergius,
Ф. 304), ms M. 8657
Moscow, late 14th or early 15th century
Parchment 32.2×24.8 cm (12⅝×9¾ in.); miniature
circular, diameter 17 cm (6⅝ in.)
300 ff., 8 miniatures

The Angel seems to float in a golden atmosphere held within the circular
frame. The sweeping stride, the flowing garments and upraised wings lend
movement, lightness and grace to the figure. The composition enclosed within
the ideal form of a circle, the light-saturated colours, the limpid sky-blues, the
combination of cool shades of blue and violet against a luminous deep gold
background, all suggest the harmony of heaven.

The facial type and the poetic treatment of the image, with its delicacy and
gentleness, are closely reminiscent of the art of Rublev.

38 The Khitrovo Lectionary
St Mark, f. 81v

Lenin Library, Moscow (transferred from the
collection of the Trinity Monastery of St Sergius,
Ф. 304), ms M. 8657
Moscow, late 14th or early 15th century
Parchment 32.2×24.8 cm (12⅝×9¾ in.); miniature
22×17 cm (8⅝×6⅝ in.)
300 ff., 8 miniatures

The miniatures of the Khitrovo Lectionary are distinguished by a lyrical, soft manner.

The slightly rounded faces of the Evangelists, with their domed foreheads, deep-set eyes and small features, are reminiscent of Andrei Rublev's favourite facial type, which often appears in his frescoes such as those in the Cathedral of the Dormition at Vladimir.

Stylistically the miniatures are based on Byzantine models, but they have an expressiveness that is their own. Among the features recurring in these miniatures are the ample robes of the saints, their rounded outlines and flowing movements. The colours are light and transparent, with hardly any modelling, and the lines are thin and delicate. Blue and gold are predominant in the bright and joyous colour-range, with two main shades of blue – a cool sky-blue for the Angel and a typically Rublevian milky (or smoky) blue for St Mark.

This style was common to both Russian and Balkan art in the early fifteenth century. Andrei Rublev was the Russian artist who brought the style to perfection, endowing it with expressiveness and symbolic meaning.

39 The Khitrovo Lectionary
St Luke, f. 102v

Lenin Library, Moscow (transferred from the
collection of the Trinity Monastery of St Sergius,
Φ. 304), ms M. 8657
Moscow, late 14th or early 15th century
Parchment 32.2×24.8 cm (12⅝×9¾ in.); miniature
21.5×16.8 cm (8¾×6½ in.)
300 ff., 8 miniatures

All the miniatures in the Khitrovo Lectionary (Pls. 36–9) are by the same
illuminator, and their similarities are naturally greater than their differences.
They have in common certain characteristics of style, the facial types depicted
and their general atmosphere. The artist is distinguished by his skill and his
mood of inner contemplation. Each portrayal, however, displays a slightly
different approach. The pious face of St Matthew (Pl. 36) is closest to Rublev's
favourite types. St Mark (Pl. 38) shows most clearly the lyrical aspect of this
style – gentleness, tender serenity and concord. St Luke is more austere and
restrained, and closer to the classical model, with a strictly geometrical system
of highlights, accentuated and rather stiff folds of the drapery, and a cold
radiance of violets and blues, favourite colours of Byzantine artists.

Rublev – if it was indeed he who painted these miniatures – was well-
acquainted with Byzantine art, which formed a basis for his work; yet Byzantine models were modified in his painting to express a profound spirituality
and a new humanity. He was one of the greatest artists of his time, not in Russia
only, but the entire Orthodox world.

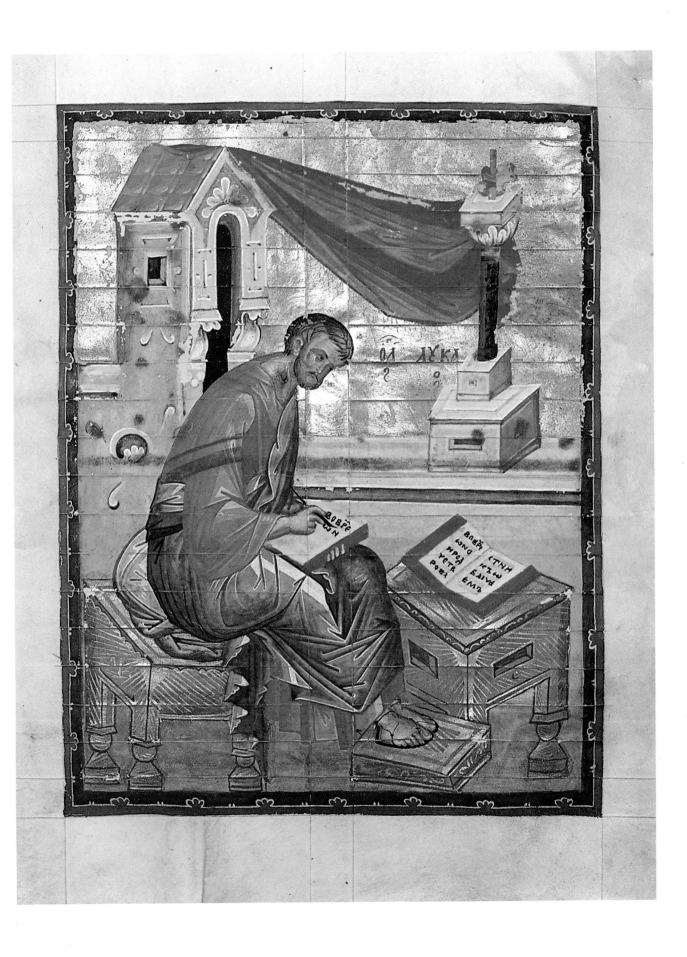

40 The Acts of the Apostles

The Apostle James (between ff. 63 and 64)

The Russian Museum, Leningrad, ms Др. гр. 20
Moscow, first third of 15th century
Parchment 27×20.5 cm (10⅝×8 in.); miniature
18.8×12.5 cm (7⅜×4⅞ in.)
265 ff. plus 7 ff. without page numbers, 6 miniatures

This large manuscript was produced in one of the workshops of Moscow. It came to the Russian Museum in 1923 from the St Cyril Monastery in Belozerye, but its previous history is unknown. It is probable that it was presented to the monastery by Prince Andrei Dmitriyevich of Mozhaisk (1382–1432), who often visited Moscow and was fond of books. He may well have purchased this manuscript.

The manuscript contains six miniatures showing the Apostles Luke, James, Peter, John, Jude and Paul. The numerous and illogically disposed architectural motifs have not yet assumed the purely decorative character they would have later in the fifteenth century, and still produce a spatial effect. The ample robes with small folds are elegantly and fancifully draped, and like the architecture, are out of scale with other parts of the composition.

The colour, although still saturated as in most fourteenth-century miniatures, is lacking in depth, and already shows a tendency towards tonal unity, typical of the later fifteenth century. Among the faces in the six miniatures, some conform to the Rublev type, tender and calm, while others are of a different type, nervous and agitated. This variation of facial types can probably be accounted for by the fact that, besides Rublev, there were a number of artists working in Russia at the time who had not yet adopted the unified style that emerged in the second half of the fifteenth century.

This manuscript was created after the Khitrovo Lectionary (Pls. 36–9) and the famous Rublev works, and its miniatures show the influence of the best works of the preceding period, both Byzantine and Russian – and particularly those of Rublev; but at the same time, they look somewhat dry, foreshadowing the emergence of a stereotyped 'grand style'.

41 The Four Gospels
St John, f. 251v

Saltykov-Shchedrin Public Library, Leningrad
(transferred from the collection of the St Cyril
Monastery in Belozerye), ms 44/49
Moscow, written last third of 15th century;
miniatures first half of 15th century
Paper 29.5×20.5 cm (11½×8 in.); miniature
17.3×11.7 cm (6¾×4½ in.)
328 ff., 4 miniatures

St John is shown writing his Gospel among the mountains, outlined against the mouth of a cave, and without St Prochoros who is usually depicted beside him. His head is turned heavenwards; his pose is tense, his gaze anxious. A sharp light illuminates the Saint's face and robes, accentuating their angularity. The irregular, broken lines contribute to the overall mystical atmosphere.

This style of depiction is far removed from the harmonious and flowing style that was predominant in fifteenth-century Russian painting. The miniatures in this manuscript are much closer to Byzantine art, or to Russian late fourteenth-century art. While examples of this style are still encountered in the beginning of the fifteenth century, the time of Andrei Rublev, they practically cease after 1430, and this consideration, as well as the miniature's similarity to those of the Acts of the Apostles of the preceding illustration (Pl. 40), suggest that it may have been painted during the first third of the fifteenth century.

42 The Ladder to Paradise of St John Climacus

The Ladder, f. 2

Lenin Library, Moscow (Desnitsky collection,
Ф. 439), ms 21, 1
Moscow, first third of 15th century
Paper 20.4×13.3 cm (8×5⅛ in.); miniature
16.4×12.1 cm (6½×4⅝ in.)
431 ff., 2 miniatures

PROVENANCE

Early history unknown; private collection of
Prof. Vasily Desnitsky (1878–1958); 1962, acquired
for the MSS Department of the Lenin Library,
Moscow, with the Desnitsky collection

At top left is an explanatory inscription: 'The Ladder. Image of the Monk's Life'. The miniature illustrates *The Ladder to Paradise*, a treatise by St John Climacus (seventh century) dealing with the religious discipline of the monk, the various forms of ascetic exercise, and the degrees of self-improvement and penance, leading to the attainment of moral perfection and the soul's ascent to heaven. This process is symbolized by a ladder of thirty rungs, to be climbed by the faithful who wish to enter the gates of heaven. The righteous are welcomed at the top by Christ, while those who have failed in the test and succumbed to temptation, fall into hell, the gaping maw of a dragon.

The naively allegorical iconography gives visual expression to the main idea of St John Climacus' Homilies. Originating in Byzantine art, it came to be widely used in Russian miniature and icon painting.

The dynamic figures, sketchily outlined, the vigorous gestures, the muted colouring, the atmosphere of drama and the underlying idea of asceticism are all features of late fourteenth-century painting and continued in early fifteenth-century art.

43 Lectionary
St John and St Prochoros, f. 1v

Historical Museum, Moscow, ms 364
Moscow, mid-15th century
Parchment 29.8×23 cm (11⅝×9 in.); miniature
26×20 cm (10⅛×7⅞ in.)
252 ff., 4 miniatures

PROVENANCE

*1890 donated to the Historical Museum by
Ye. Sheremetyeva*

While the manuscript contains no notes relating to its creation, it was undoubtedly produced in Moscow, between 1430 and 1450, or perhaps a few years later.

That the manuscript is written on parchment makes it a rarity for its time, because from the middle of the fifteenth century almost all manuscripts in Russia were written on paper. To use parchment instead of paper was by then an extravagance, so the manuscript must have been produced at the special request of the patron.

The miniatures portraying the Four Evangelists are executed in a manner typical of the Moscow school, and immediately recall those of the Acts of the Apostles (Pl. 40). However, the miniatures of the present manuscript display slightly different stylistic features. Architectural backgrounds are reduced to flat, decorative shapes and landscape to two-dimensional, seemingly weightless piles of rocks, coloured pale mauve or blue-green and reminiscent of an exquisite stage-set. The figures are elongated and fragile, the colours light and transparent, with practically no modelling by highlights. The outlines are simpler and more decorative here than in the manuscripts of the preceding period. The Saints' pious faces with small features conform to the early fifteenth-century type, but they are less profound. The softness of manner and delicacy of forms foreshadow the emergence of a new style, one which was to predominate in the second half of the fifteenth century.

44 The Four Gospels

St Luke, f. 150v

Lenin Library, Moscow (transferred from the
collection of the Moscow Theological Academy,
Φ. 173), ms 1
Moscow, last third of 15th century
Paper 31×20.5 cm (12⅛×8 in.); miniature 21×15 cm
(8¼×5⅞ in.)
317 ff., 4 miniatures

PROVENANCE

*Library of the Trinity Monastery of St Sergius; 1742
the Trinity Theological Seminary; 1814 transferred to
the Moscow Theological Academy; 1930 transferred
to Lenin Library, Moscow*

The manuscript from the library of the Trinity Monastery of St Sergius may
either have been created in a Moscow scriptorium and transferred to the
monastery, or have been written in the monastery itself. The monastery
evidently had its own scriptorium with expert scribes and illuminators who
emulated the best examples of the Moscow school.

The miniatures are permeated with a soft lyricism and a spirit of calm
contemplation. The faces of the Evangelists recall Rublev's subtle facial types
devoid of strongly manifested emotion. The Evangelists express the Orthodox
Christian type of spirituality, characterized by harmony and peace and a total
absence of external signs of exaltation; in this the illuminators closely follow
Rublev.

The lines are gently curved, the contours flowing; the ample robes seem to
envelop the figures. The proportions are without emphasis, the colours soft
and tender. The architectural backgrounds, recalling Byzantine compositions,
serve a purely decorative function. Here we find a world of ideal harmony,
removed from all mundane associations.

45 Book of the Prophets (with commentaries)

The Prophet Zachariah, f. 71v

Lenin Library, Moscow (transferred from the
collection of the Moscow Theological Academy,
Φ. 173), ms 20
Moscow, 1489
Paper 31.5×20.5 cm (12⅜×8 in.); miniature
23.2×15.2 cm (9⅛×5⅞ in.)
349 ff., 18 miniatures

PROVENANCE

Library of the Trinity Monastery of St Sergius; 1742
the Trinity Theological Seminary; 1814 the Moscow
Theological Academy; 1930 transferred to Lenin
Library, Moscow

This large volume comprises the texts of the sixteen prophetic books of the Old
Testament with commentaries, and contains sixteen miniatures portraying the
Prophets. The scribe's note on folio 1 indicates that the work on the book,
commissioned by the Deacon Vasiliy Mamyrev, was completed on 25 December 1489.

The Book of the Prophets will have been executed in the Kremlin scriptorium by a competent scribe and several illuminators. The artist who portrayed Zachariah is among the best Moscow artists of his time: some art historians even go so far as to suggest the hand of Dionisy, the outstanding painter who worked in Moscow around 1500. But the miniature could well have been created by some other Moscow artist who painstakingly imitated that painter's style.

The tall, light figure of Zachariah, with small head and narrow feet, is presented in an S-shaped pose and seems to be floating above the ground. The face is executed in a technique which consists in applying transparent layers of ochre of differing shades, imperceptibly merging to create a subtle and complex colour-variation. The method was widely used in icon painting of the Moscow school in the late fifteenth century, but was rarely employed in the small-scale art of book illumination. In this miniature, the almost imperceptible fusion of shades of brown seems eminently suitable to convey the state of inner spiritual contemplation of the Prophet.

The pose and proportions of the figure are reminiscent of the early fourteenth-century painting of the Chora Monastery at Constantinople, and of the frescoes of late fourteenth- and early fifteenth-century Moravian school, still surviving in Ravanica, Resava and Kalenić in Yugoslavia. This style is revived in Moscow in the fifteenth century in the art of Dionisy and his followers.

46 Biblical Miscellany

The Archangel Gabriel and Moses in the Desert, f. 2v

Lenin Library, Moscow (acquired with the
Undolsky collection, Ф. 310), ms 1
Moscow (?), last quarter of 15th century (probably
between 1480 and 1490); compiled and written by
Ivan Chorny
Paper 32×20.5 cm (12½×8 in.); miniature
22.8×13.5 cm (8⅞×5¼ in.)
476 ff., 1 miniature

Provenance

*1840–60s collection of V. Undolsky, Russian scholar
and palaeographer; 1866 the Undolsky collection
acquired by Moscow Public Museum; after 1917
manuscripts of the former Undolsky collection
transferred to Lenin Library, Moscow*

This manuscript containing a miscellany of texts, mainly taken from the books of the Bible, was compiled and written by Ivan Chorny, known in fifteenth-century Russia as a professional scribe working under the patronage of Ivan III (1462–1505). The book opens with the one miniature of the volume. Its subject is unique. It shows Moses with the Archangel Gabriel, who holds a scroll on which is inscribed the legend that Gabriel, the Lord's messenger, is bringing to Moses the command of the Almighty to learn 'the teachings of God on the creation of heaven, earth and all flesh', and to write these teachings down. The quotation is not from the Old Testament but from *The Tale of Bygone Years*, an Old Russian chronicle written between 1111 and 1113. This tells the story of Moses' escape to Midian and his wanderings in the desert, where he 'learned from the Archangel Gabriel all concerning the creation of the world and of man ... the Flood and the confusion of tongues ... the motions of the stars ... and how to count and how to measure land, and numberless other wise things'. So the miniature introduces the wisdom to follow in the selections from the Old Testament.

Ivan Chorny himself, in his notes in the margins, offers his own commentary on texts which seem to need elucidation.

47 The Sermons of St Gregory the Great

St Gregory the Great, St Sophia and the Archdeacon Peter, f. 1v

Lenin Library, Moscow (acquired with the
Ovchinnikov collection), ms 794
Novgorod (?), Moscow (?), late 15th century
Paper 19.7×13.3 cm (7¾×5⅛ in.); miniature
17.3×11 cm (6¾×4⅜ in.)
247 ff., 1 miniature

PROVENANCE

*19th century, collection of P. Ovchinnikov, a
merchant and collector of manuscripts; 1919
acquired for Lenin Library, Moscow*

This small manuscript, of unassuming appearance and written on paper, opens
with a miniature portraying St Gregory the Great with his pupil the Archdeacon Peter. Behind St Gregory is St Sophia, Divine Wisdom, represented as
an Angel, inspiring St Gregory while remaining invisible to him. The history
of the manuscript is unknown. Some features, however, seem to point to
Novgorod as its place of origin. Among these are the presence of St Sophia,
characteristic of fifteenth- and sixteenth-century Novgorod manuscripts, and
the facial types, common in late fifteenth-century Novgorod icons, as well as
the thick layers of saturated colours and the solid forms which distinguish
Novgorod painting.

Certain other features – the delicate, almost pretty, faces, the elongated
proportions, the flowing lines and the high and light architectural forms –
seem, rather, to point to Moscow. One must remember, however, that the
Moscow style, which was becoming increasingly the Russian style, reached
Novgorod in the late fifteenth century, so that there was intermingling of the
original Novgorodian traditions and Moscow tastes in the works of Novgorodian artists.

The miniature has been restored and shows traces of darkened oil.

48 The Theodosios Gospels
St Mark, f. 109v

Saltykov-Shchedrin Public Library, Leningrad
(acquired with the Pogodin collection), ms 133
Moscow, 1507
Paper 27×19 cm (10⅝×7⅜ in.); miniature
17×12.5 cm (6⅝×4⅞ in.)
381 ff., 4 miniatures

PROVENANCE

*Collection of M. Pogodin; 1852 transferred to Public
Library, St Petersburg*

Noted for its lavish and exquisite decoration, this manuscript created in
Moscow at the very beginning of the sixteenth century already differs considerably from fifteenth-century manuscripts in its general appearance and the
style of its miniatures and ornament. The early sixteenth century, marked by
the development of new artistic ideas, was a turning-point for both Russian
icon painting and the art of book illumination.

We know the names of the artists who worked on the decoration of these
Gospels. The miniatures were painted by Theodosios, the son of Dionisy, one
of the greatest Russian painters (*cf.* Pl. 45), and were decorated with gold by an
artist named Mikhail Medovartsov, who was also responsible for the fine
ornamentation, composed mainly of delicate gold patterning.

The miniatures are so exquisite in detail, and contain such a wealth of
ornamental elements that they suggest the art of the jeweller rather than the
painter. The fifteenth-century tradition can still be observed in the facial types,
the flowing contours, the softly modelled drapery and the general atmosphere
of refinement and harmony, but there is also a new tendency towards sumptuous decorativeness. The miniatures are overfilled with toy-like architecture;
ornamental backgrounds have taken the place of the earlier plain gold ones; the
text is often incorporated into the ornament. Three-dimensionality is gone; the
colours are brighter and have lost their characteristic smoky quality and
transparency. The former sense of intimacy and lyricism gives place to outward brilliance. The faces, while retaining the traditional rendering of the
features, no longer convey the impression of profound inner contemplation.
The images have grown more superficial.

The miniatures created by Theodosios mark the end of an important stage of
Russian painting spanning the fifteenth century, and stand at the beginning of a
new artistic period.

Марко съиньшеседмидесѧтноучникъ. петрꙋапⷭлоⷡпостꙋ
пленъбꙑиепⷭⷦпъвьалезаньрїн. весьмнⷧюбѧше. исⷮꙋ
птаньꙑисⷬⷶти. нꙋместъ еꙉлїанаписавь. нтѣмꙋ
ченїаконецьпрїѧтъ. распѧтъвнамаслинꙋнѣ.꙰⁘—